DIAMOND IN THE ROUGH

Refining Inner Beauty through Emotional Healing

Laurette Taylor Johnson

Jawbone Publishing Corporation   Kissimmee, FL

www.JawbonePublishing.com

copyright©2005 by Laurette Taylor Johnson

2907 Paddington Way
Kissimmee, FL 34747
407-396-4245
www.JawbonePublishing.com

Printed in the United States of America

All scriptural references are from the Amplified Bible, publishedd by Zondervan, Grand Rappids. MI, and copyrighted©1987 by the Zondervan Corporation and the Lockman Foundation.

No part of this book may be reproduced or transmitted in any form or by any means, electronic or mechanical, including photocopying, recording, or any information storage and retrieval system now known or to be invented, without permission in writing from the author, except by a reviewer in connection with a review or inclusion in a magazine, newspaper, or broadcast.

Table of Contents

	Introduction	5
1.	Momma and Me	7
2.	No Father But God *Protracted Grieving*	27
3.	Children are God's Heritage	41
4.	No Greater Love *Severing Unhealthy Ties*	*49*
5.	Victim of Rape	55
6.	Heart Beyond Prison Bars	65
7.	Grandchildren	73
8.	Stepmother's Woes	81
9.	Dark Valley Days *Physical Illness*	*91*
10.	Java and a Friend	103
11.	Overweight? *Perfectionism*	*111*
12.	God's Gift Unopened *Abortion*	*117*
13.	Men Ought to Pause *Menopause*	*127*
14.	Who Am I? *Identity Crisis*	*145*
15.	Take the Scenic Route	153
16.	Body, Soul, and Spirit	161
17.	Happy on Purpose	169
18.	Fair Maiden and her Prince	179

Acknowledgments

A special thanks to the love of my life, Willie, who is my counselor and writing coach, for his gift of wisdom to me in the compilation of my thoughts in writing this book.

I would also like to thank my sons, Kelton, Michael, Curtis, Jr., and my daughter, Angela, for weathering the storms of life with me.

And a special thanks to my editor/publisher, Swanee Ballman (a God-send) of Jawbone Publishing., for the refinement and luminosity of **Diamond in the Rough**.

God bless,

Laurette

Introduction

The diamond, in its original state, is one of the hardest substances known to mankind. In order for its exquisite beauty to be revealed, it has to go through a process of cutting, sawing, and cleaving to eradicate any flaws. Once this process is completed and perfected, not only does it display great beauty; it is also priceless.

Similarly, a woman is like a *diamond in the rough*. Beneath the emotional rubbish that lies dormant in her soul is a priceless inner beauty—waiting to be exposed.

By the masses, women are suffering emotionally, and many of us have spent most of our lives plagued with guilt and regrets. We ponder, *I ought to have done this, or I ought to have done that,* while rearing our children. Had we made better decisions and been better parents (*we muse*), perhaps they would not be experiencing such difficulties in life.

This may be partially, but not entirely true. Our adult children are separate individuals with their own strength of will, and they (not us) must be held responsible for their choices.

As parents, we generally give our children the type of love and nurturing that we received from our parents. Likewise, our parents (for the most part) reared us as they were reared. But there is no such thing as the perfect parent—imperfection did not originate with us, nor did our parents instigate it. Adam and Eve set the fallen nature of mankind in motion, in the Garden of Eden. That was long before any of our ancestors or us was even born. (In Genesis, God gave Adam and Eve permission to eat of every tree in the garden — except the forbidden tree. But they disobeyed God's command, and overtime the entire world was hurled into a sinful state.)

Diamond in the Rough is composed of information that will set women free from their emotional bondages. I have stripped down to my bare soul, and my heart has bled upon its pages. There were times I struggled with pride and was tempted not to write about my life. But the temptation was aborted and replaced with the satisfaction of knowing that others may experience healing through my life's tragedies.

Many women have spent half-lives filled with guilt, and they find it difficult to forgive themselves. When we fail to forgive ourselves or accept God's forgiveness, we become open prey to tormentors (including fear, guilt, anxiety, restlessness, sickness, dis-ease, and self-hatred).

Do not fall prey to the lies and deception of the enemy; self-condemnation does not atone for our past mistakes, nor is it a noble gesture. The nobility lies in what Jesus has done for us. He has declared us not guilty before God. We were placed in right standing with God through the gift of His Son. When we continue to live a life plagued with feelings of guilt, we disobey God's command to forgive (ourselves).

Momma and Me

"Momma and Me" was written to explain the correlation between mothers and daughters. And to bring about a better understanding of what a significant role mothers play in their daughter's lives.

As daughters, we tend to emulate the learned behavioral patterns of our mothers. We then transpose that same behavioral pattern to our own daughters.

There is a great deal of truth to the old saying "like mother, like daughter" (although some of us are less than happy to admit it and often with good reason). Many daughters have been discouraged and greatly disappointed in much of what they have seen in their mothers' lives. And as they grow older, they fight like the dickens to be different from the way their mothers were.

On average, daughter's lives run parallel to their mother's lives.

***

Despite our best efforts, none of us come out of a dysfunctional home totally unscathed. In some cases there is an obvious portrayal of a mother by her daughter, and in others, a subtle similarity. Henry Ward Beecher said, *"The mother's heart is the child's schoolroom."* Generally, a mother is the most influential person in her impressionable daughter's life.

It is unlikely that a mother will intentionally teach her daughter to mimic her negative attributes. However, much of what we have seen has been subliminally stored in our memory banks. Therefore, in order to eradicate our emotional flaws, it's imperative that we get a clear-cut understanding of what has actually transpired in our lives.

Although I'm from the same dough, I chose a different shape cookie cutter.

* * *

The northwest section of the city of Hallandale, Florida, exemplified that of a great community in the 50's. Folks did not just live next door; they were genuinely hospitable neighbors who intermingled with one another. The children were accountable to most of the adults who, for the most part, we both respected and revered. Meeting a stranger was almost unheard of during those times.

As a community we did many things together, including worship. There were not churches on every street corner or in every storefront. Although there were a few, we simply congregated at the nearest church.

Collectively, countless people make one voice to praise one God.

* * *

The most lucrative businesses in our black section of town were the number-runners (houses where folks gambled), and the neighborhood stores. The storeowners sold big, round, two-for-one penny Smiling Jack, Coconut, and Butter cookies. As well as, Mary Jane, Squirrel Nut and Cherry candies, which were hard to chew but absolutely toothsome.

Since we were such a close knit community, even children were allowed to purchase cigarettes for their parents. But if our parents did not get their cigarettes for whatever reason, our hind parts would pay dearly.

Were those really the good old days?

* * *

Momma and I lived in a dilapidated, weather-beaten house with peeling white paint trimmed in faded green. Large chips of paint that had separated from the rotted wood often lay on the ground nearby.

Aluminum shutters spanned the entire front porch. We manually lifted them because the cranks were broken. As Momma opened them every morning, the sun's rays illuminated the entire porch.

Slipping out from under the warm bedcovers, I stumbled sleepy-eyed to the dinning room / porch (which were one in the same) and flopped down on one of the mixed match chairs.

Even more than a condition of life, poverty is a state of mind.

* * *

Approximately three steps from our dinning room and a quick right turn was our tiny kitchen. The counter was made of a wooden flat board securely prompted with sticks. Tin basins were used as sinks to wash and rinse the dishes. Like clockwork, about 7:00 a.m. Momma came from the kitchen, placing before me a bowl of hot oatmeal.

The lump of butter and pile of sugar on top looked nauseating and I had no intentions whatsoever of eating it. But seeing as Momma had gone through the trouble of preparing it, I thought it best to make some use of it. So I sat and played in it while I watched her go through her morning ritual to prepare for work, which was far more interesting than my oatmeal.

Typically, daughters are their mother's greatest fans.

***

The most amusing times of those uneventful mornings was watching the special care Momma took in making her coffee. The whistling sound of the lopsided pot alerted the water had come to full boil. Predictably, she added one heaping spoonful of Instant Maxwell House coffee, a dash of sugar, and Carnation milk. To get her desired temperature, she added one large cube of ice. I loved watching her sip it, as though she really did enjoy it to the very last drop. Meanwhile, her ashtray would gradually fill with the buds of her Philip Morris cigarettes, each of which bore a ring from her burgundy colored lipstick.

What daughters see daughters do!

***

What was on Momma's mind? I often wondered to myself as she stared out of those old broken shutters while chain smoking her cigarettes. Perhaps she thought of the many times she left her little girl at home alone while attending another woman's offspring. Or maybe she was taken aback by the thought of scrubbing the floors of someone else's mansion, while her own wooden floors were making unambiguous threats of caving in. How incredibly beautiful she was to me in her white starched uniform dress.

Her legs crossed, the wooden floors creaking beneath her polished white loafers.

Heavy are the burdens that press like dumb bells upon a mother's heart.

***

Doubtless ingrained in me as a child, I still struggle with smoking from time to time. Fortunately, I did not smoke when my children were growing up. This may account for the fact that most of them do not (with the exception of one son, whose father was a frequent smoker). However, in growing older, I have found the temptation a bit overwhelming at times.

Like mother, like daughter?

***

Watching my mother apply her makeup was one of my favorite pastimes. Her pecan complexion looked flawless with her nutmeg brown face powder. For blusher, she smoothed her black orchid (dark burgundy) lipstick across her defined cheekbones to enhance them. Similar to Momma's, I wear a spice brown face powder and a burgundy shade of lipstick, which I also use to enhance my cheeks.

I mimicked Momma, not just in the way she looked but also the way she lived.

***

At the honking of Miss Evelyn's horn, Momma rushed out of the house to go to work. Meanwhile, I would mosey along to my elementary school, which was a short distance from our home. Unlike Momma, I was in no particular hurry, knowing fully the cruel mocking I would endure from my schoolmates. They loved reminding me of what a shabby house I lived in, as though there were any remote possibility that I could ever forget. Then there were other times that I actually waited until the last bell rang before scurrying to school. On those mornings I was usually late, which is another pattern that I developed and have not yet thoroughly conquered.

With time and practice, negative habits are perfected.

***

The run-down cars that Momma owned were as old as our house, which gave the kids another reason to tease me. The junior high school that I later attended was a lot further and whenever I was running late (which was most of the times), Momma was generous enough to give me a lift in our jalopy. In order to keep the kids from seeing me, I would stoop down on the floor of the car.

On one unforgettable day, the most embarrassing thing happened. A foul mouthed, mean girl (that nothing short of exorcism could have helped) saw me sneak a look from the back seat.

Overcoming the opinions of others, will defuse most our fears.

***

I never wanted to hurt Momma. Although I was young, I somehow knew she was doing her best. She knew that the kids often teased me, so instead of putting me out directly in front of the school, she dropped me off up the street. The moment my feet hit the soil of the campus grounds, the demon-possessed girl impatiently blurted, "Laurette, I saw your momma bringing you to school in that old raggedy car."

And just as I suspected by the end of the day, the other kids enthusiastically shared in her humor—at my expense. Being poor had many disadvantages, and the endless taunting was devastating.

Lack of nurturing or verbal expression of love damages us emotionally.

***

Eventually, it seems Momma gave up altogether and refused to purchase another car. Instead she used public transportation or paid someone to give her a ride.

In retrospect, I deeply regret making life even more difficult for Momma. But I was so overtaken with shame that I could not see beyond my own pain. Still, I believe she understood perfectly what I had to contend with. Any time the kids came over to play stickball, she would bring us out some popcorn, sweet bread, and lemonade, made with fresh lemons from our tree...her way, no doubt, of trying to recruit new friends for me.

Mothers are not perfect, but most have perfectly good intentions.

***

The fruit trees were plentiful and practically surrounded our diminutive house.

Happily, I would dash barefoot across the sun-baked sand and prickly weeds to indulge myself when the fruits were in season. Climbing faster than any boy could, I steadied myself on one of the cherry tree limbs, and ate until my stomach was well satisfied. Equally tantalizing were the fruit from the coconut, sugar apple, sapodilla and avocado trees.

The same trees that were delectable by day provoked fear after dark. The huge limbs brushed rudely against the house, casting oversized shadows through the windows. The strange noises were no less than haunting. And if that were not ghastly enough, after I had fallen asleep Momma would go up the street to the neighborhood bar.

Insecure girls grow up to be insecure women.

***

Many nights I awakened in the pitch dark house alone and panicked. This left me with one of two options: either stay at home and be tormented by the creaking, crackling sounds of the haunted house, or run at the speed of lightening to my neighbor's house, possibly subjecting myself to rejection. I chose the latter. When Momma came home and found me gone, she would be terribly embarrassed to come and retrieve me.

Fear of rejection in the heart of an adult, took up residency during their childhood.

***

Our doors could not lock and virtually anyone could have walked in on me. But, thank God we were a community, and people were not committing the malicious and heinous crimes that they are today. Still, I had difficulty falling asleep at night, as I would almost expect Momma to be gone when I had awakened. Many years later, I too eventually left my children at home while I went night clubbing. Although the doors were securely locked, things were considerably worse than when I was growing up.

Can you see the pattern?

***

My mother was about five years of age when her mother died. Momma never got the nurturing and affirmation from her mother to prepare her for motherhood. My grandfather (Papa) reared Momma and her three siblings alone. Seemingly, she adopted some of his mannerisms... *like father, like daughter*. Papa was said to have been a good provider and strict disciplinarian, but had difficulty expressing his emotions. Although she hardly ever disciplined me, Momma was a good provider, but emotionally inexpressive.

What most parents were—their children are.

***

The legacy of the cruel and unjust treatment of Southern blacks during slavery times was also patterned by those who were either directly or indirectly affected by it. Many of the men slaves were sold by their masters and sent to other plantations under a new slave owner. This left their families (and more importantly, their sons) without a role model. With all that the men had gone through themselves, they may not have been able to depict a strong father image. Be that as it may, some type of role model may have been better than none.

Why are there so many broken homes in the black community?

***

The women also suffered in that they were used at will for the sexual pleasure of their slave owners. Today many of our children have different fathers, not because we craved sex, but were hungry for true love. We had been taught that men only desired our bodies—not us...confirming the fact that learned behavior is passed on from one generation to the next. The insufferable abuse endured by Southern black slave women, in many cases was the legacy passed on to their descendants.

There's more to me than the eye can see.

***

The crude and merciless way some elderly black folks punished their children in many ways depicted the after math of slavery. It was common for some children to be beaten with palmetto sticks, electrical cords or hit with their parents' fist in their mouths. This sounds a lot like what was practiced during slavery times. I reiterate the purpose of this chapter is for healing, not to cast blame.

Often, before soaring into the future, we have to journey back into our past.

***

As a girl, I learned from Momma how to care for the elderly, sick and shut-in. I spent much of my time running to their homes taking food she had sent. An elderly gentleman who lived on our block seemed especially delighted to see me approaching with brown paper bag in hand. The old man always wore the same baggy suspender pants, a long - sleeve shirt (regardless of the weather), and a gray hat. His beard was gray and scraggly, and his pipe hung on his bottom lip. He sat in his wooden rocker every day glaring at passersby from his porch.

God gives to us, through us.

***

Due to his failing eyesight, the elderly gentleman would bring his chair to a squeaking halt, so that he could identify the oncoming intruder. Smiling from ear to ear, he was overjoyed at the prospect of Ms. Eseline sending him some scrumptious, finger-licking soul food. She sent smothered pork chops, chicken or stewed beef, along with pigeon peas and rice, potato salad, cornbread and a slice of homemade cake.

How amazing she was, out of her little she gave to others who were less fortunate.

A blessing is like a boomerang; it always returns.

***

For the parties at school, I was elected hands down to bring one of Momma's homemade cakes. She was well known by my classmates for her peppermint, pecan, and pineapple upside down cakes.

Momma was truly incredible in many ways. Every so often, she would pack a picnic basket and after Sunday service, off to the beach we went. And *whenever,* Mr. Sidney Poitier starred in a movie, we would definitely be spending that Saturday at the matinee. As an adolescent, naturally I was not as appreciative of Mr. Poitier, as I had grown to be in later years, but the refreshments made up for that misfortune. And rain or shine, Sunday morning we went to church, which was not optional.

Let us remember not to forget the good times.

***

There were a few churches in our immediate neighborhood. We were faithful members of St. Annie's Episcopal church, which my grandfather co-founded. However, the church right around the corner seemed far more lively and interesting than ours. Most people in our community called it the *sanctified church,* where old women wore long, white dresses, with linen cloths on their heads, and black string up shoes that looked like army boots.

Holiness is not worn on our heads, but in our hearts.

The *sanctified women* (as we called them) would beat on old tin washtubs for drums and slap tambourines up and down against their hands while stomping their feet and doing a holiness dance. Out of curiosity, some of the neighborhood kids would peep through any opening that we could find in the drapes. I remember thinking those old sanctified ladies were sure candidates to get through the pearly gates of heaven. Many nights when they apparently caught the spirit, the entire neighborhood would be kept awake for most of the night. Nevertheless, I feared God (out of ignorance) and would not have dared to murmur against what I later learned might have been...*a noisy gong or a clanging cymbal (I Corinthian 13:1).*

***

Next to St. Annie's was our Parish Hall, where the members bought and ate breakfast after service. The smell of bacon and coffee often made its way through the church's stained-glass windows, making it difficult for me, if for no one else to concentrate on the service in session.

Momma faithfully took her turn cooking on Sunday mornings, and usually prepared boiled fish and grits with hot buttered biscuits. Whenever she cooked, I was guaranteed a hearty breakfast. After service most of the members would gather at the Parish Hall for chitchat while they ate. Meanwhile, Momma would have her own dinner cooking at home on a low fire.

There is a thin line separating wholesome chitchat from idol gossip.

***

We lived across the street from the church and Momma wanted her dinner done by the time we returned home. One Sunday morning a neighbor ran to the church and informed Momma that her house was on fire. Moments later, the entire sanctuary emptied. Spectators scurried onto the streets to see the alleged burning house. Perhaps some were genuinely concerned, but others merely wanted to see a sideshow. Smoke had filled our house, but by God's grace it had not caught on fire.

As I looked up at Momma's face, her shame was easily identifiable—I wore it daily.

People, who don't have your best interest at heart, should not be on your mind.

∗∗∗

Momma had a huge void in her life and an unquenchable thirst for love. She sought desperately (mostly in the wrong places), to fill it. More times than not, the life that's lived before us is to some degree replicated by us. In pursuit of love, for a brief time she apparently thought to have found it in my father. He was said to be quite the lady's man back in his day and the most eligible bachelor around town. My father saw my mother standing out in the yard wearing shorts that revealed her shapely legs. He was instantly captivated.

Our beauty is often valued by others, but undervalued by us.

∗∗∗

Daddy decided to make a smooth move on her, but did not know that Momma was no small change. Eseline Morgan had it going on. She was striking to look at and had a voluptuous figure. Daddy's best mack was to catch and clean a raccoon, and Momma's was to prepare it gourmet style. They ate and fell in love at first bite. But since they were two emotionally deficient people, the relationship would not last very long.

Most broken people find it easy to come together, but hard to stay together. Daddy had never known his biological father and said his stepfather heartlessly rejected him. Leaving home at an early age, Daddy said he eventually learned to hop freight trains, and took up gambling as a way of survival. When he met Momma they were two lonely people trying to fill each other's voids. Later I was added to their broken equation.

How can a man without a role model find his way?

***

Desperately wanting Momma's approval, I became an overachiever at school.

I eagerly volunteered to participate in as many school activities as possible. Spelling contests, school dances, assembly plays and track and field. I tried them all...and generally finished among the top three contenders. I wanted desperately to hear Momma say you did well, or you're smart, but, mostly, *I love you!*

Every week she washed and straightened my hair, making me nice long ponytails, but I never remember her telling me afterwards that I was pretty. Her vocabulary seemed void of such words; perhaps they had not been spoken to her.

May the love in your heart roll off the tip of your tongue.

***

During my father's travels he met and moved in with a lady in Camden, New Jersey. Momma was alone with me when I was just learning to walk. He visited me from time to time and always told me how much he loved me. However, the love he said he felt was not consistent with what he showed me.

He'd say, "Baby, I'm coming to town to see you."

Excitedly I would ask, "When? Daddy, when?"

He'd then say something like, "Saturday, baby. I'll be there Saturday two weeks from today.

A child's fragile emotions, like breakaway glass, are easily shattered!

***

After our conversation, I started counting the days on the calendar.

Finally, the day would approach when Daddy faithfully promised me he was coming. Breaking out of our front door, I ran as fast as my legs would carry me to get to grandma Ruby's house. (She was my daddy's mother and I absolutely, positively adored her.) Her smile warmly welcomed me into her heart and her home.

My grandma Ruby's home was often my haven.

***

Breathless, with sweat dripping from my sandy brown hair, I sat on my grandma's sofa sucking my salty thumb. I nervously watched the front door, as I swung my legs back and forth against the plastic that protected her furniture. I hoped desperately that my Daddy would walk through the screen door and pick me up in his big, strong arms.

Grandma Ruby would once again break the silence with words that were almost unbearable. "You child, I don't know why your daddy's such a big liar. He ain't coming."

I was accustomed to leaving Grandma's house with my heart shattered, but the pain never seemed to have gotten easier.

A broken promise is better kept than given away.

When daddy called me "his pumpkinseed" and told me he loved me, I believe he meant every word. Over time, I came to understand that he was handicapped by his gambling and alcohol addiction. Daddy's addiction not only prohibited him from living a stable lifestyle but securing me with one, as well.

Momma did whatever she had to do to make adequate provision, but showed very little affection.

I grew up pretty mixed up. As a woman, I experienced some of the same perplexities in life that they had.

Our parents did their best—it's up to us to do the rest.

***

Though Momma was beautiful, she was broken. Still, she had many admirable qualities. While I admired her beauty and kindheartedness, as a young woman I vowed not to embark on a string of broken relationships the way she had. In my initial endeavor to be different from her, I went to the opposite extreme. I refused to leave a relationship, although I was severely battered. But the baton had already passed from Momma to me. Years later I extended it to my daughter.

Don't put up with someone who's tearing you down.

***

The same correlation between mothers and daughters also apply to sons and fathers. Impressionable boys generally grow up and treat their companions the way their fathers treated their mothers. In many instances, the father who is abusive to his wife and neglects his children instills the same low morals in his son.

Customarily, sons are the depiction of their fathers.

***

Like a link in a chain, parents are connected to both their ancestors and their descendants. Our ancestors include the generation immediately before us (i.e., our parents), who have greatly influenced our lives. Likewise, we have an emotional impact on our immediate descendants, the generation after us (i.e., our children). When the chain is not secured by the adjoining links, it will not function, as it should.

What link are you in the family chain?

In the family chain, the more securely we are connected to our ancestors, the better our linkage to our descendants. Each generation passes down to the next generation what was received from the one before. For instance, I gave my children what my parents gave me. And my parents gave me what their parents gave them. And so on and so forth.

For countless generations, the family chain has been damaged. Therefore, I strongly suggest that you seek God's restorative plan for yourself, as well as the many generations of descendants that are to follow. During recovery, vacillating can and should be expected. But remain steadfast, because mending your broken lineage will be beneficial to many.

What will you pass on to your descendants?

***

This is not to discredit or show disrespect to either of my parents. I thank God for them both. I truly love my father and will always cherish the memory of my beloved mother. Nor is this an attempt to cast blame on my parents, but rather to implement an understanding that will promote healing.

Growing up, I had many of the basic external things of life, food to eat, nice clothes to wear, and pretty ribbons for my hair. But due to neglect and lack of affirmation my life was negatively impacted.

Your insufferable childhood may not have been your fault, but your emotional health is your responsibility.

Wounded Emotions

*A bruise within is but a spot or stain,
but when pressed upon, it causes excruciating pain.*

*Darkness covers it, makes it all right
but when Jesus comes in, it's under spotlight.*

That old bruise that has built a scab and become scaly and old

When under the Master's touch then becomes like pure gold.

No Father, but God

Grieving the loss of a loved one is something that everyone experiences at one time or another. It is as natural as breathing. You grieve and moan and go through life remembering the loss of someone who was near and dear to you. It is all a part of the process of healing a broken heart.

My grieving the loss of my loved ones exceeded a normal grieving process, and was as excessive as it was abnormal. For many years, I grieved the deaths of my mother, who was tragically killed, and my first-born son, who died eleven months later.

***

About two years prior to her death, Momma and I had just moved out of our old frame house into a newly constructed home. She had it built, from the ground up, in the predominantly black section of Hallandale, Florida. It was a beautiful white house trimmed in bright orange around the top and a deeper orange with sparkling brickwork around the lower front. The inside of our home was as beautiful as the outside.

Momma extravagantly decorated her room in sundry shades of purple and white. Her lavender sheers swayed back and forth as the breeze blew gently through her windows. A beautiful purple patchwork quilt on her bed charmingly complimented her room.

My room was next to Momma's. It was decorated in pink and white and was fit for a fairy tale princess. Soft pink coverlets with ruffles adorned my pink and white twin beds, and snow white curtains hung at the windows. The living room sofa wrapped around two entire walls, and beneath its sturdy oak wood legs was a matching beige carpet. In the dinning room, a glitzy chandelier with teardrop crystals danced over the cherry-wood dinette setting. At last Momma built her dream house. But just as she was preparing to live in it, she died.

***

My siblings who were much older than I had all moved out to start a life of their own. As I shared in the previous chapter, I saw very little of my father who lived up North. Like many other girls that grew up without their fathers, I had a huge void in my life. This caused me to be both vulnerable and susceptible to peer pressure. And in an attempt to fill my void, I started dating. After several months, the boy I was dating seemed discontent in our monogamous relationship. I had qualms about engaging in a sexual relationship, but it was a trade-off for the intimacy that I deeply desired.

After my brief and unpleasant encounter with sex, I immediately conceived. Shortly after, I learned that I was pregnant and unenthusiastically got married. Being young and inexperienced, we had no choice but to move in with his mother. Although I had moved out of my mother's home, I visited her daily, without fail. As I sat and watched her prepping for work, I decided that I would not disclose my troubled heart to her. In addition to being pregnant, I was also a battered wife.

Whenever Momma confronted me about things I kept from her, she would often say, "A little bird told me." And I knew it would only be a matter of time before the news flew her way. As I suspected, she did learn of my distressing situation and insisted that I moved back home. She added, "Your husband is welcome to come, if he wishes".

Actually, I found her request to be quite liberating, and she did not have to ask twice. I happily moved back home. My husband came alone, though reluctantly I am inclined to believe.

On January 19, 1970, I gave birth to James Arthur Hardwick III. We called him Poncho, and as it turned out his nickname was appropriate. He had a milky caramel complexion, slanted dark eyes and black, silky straight hair. Everyone thought that he was absolutely beautiful, and after his head (having been squeezed by my pelvic bone) was properly shaped, I thought he was pretty cute, too. Nevertheless, I must honestly confess the thought of being responsible for another human being scared the living wits out of me. After all, at seventeen, I did not even know how to take care of myself.

At night, when Poncho would cry with what I learned in later years to be colic, I thought he was spoiled. As an inexperienced mother, I had decided to break him out of it by allowing him to cry for awhile. This was inconsiderate of Momma who was sleeping in the next room, and had to go to work the following day.

"What is wrong with you, why are you letting him cry?" She blurted out angrily.

"Momma he's crying because he wants someone to pick him up" I replied defensively.

"Don't be ridiculous," she shouted back. "Crying is the only way that he can communicate something is wrong with him."

After bundling Poncho up, she took him and his belongings to her room for the rest of the night. Before long, Momma was almost completely taking care of him, which she really did not seem to mind. She utterly adored him.

Momma bought two red caps for Poncho and her, and they wore them on their excursions to town. Even though I was married, Momma was actually the one who took care of us. However, the security that Poncho and I both found in Momma would soon come to an abrupt and unexpected end.

***

Friday night, November 13, 1970, Momma left home without a word to anyone about where she was going. She was free-spirited and often came and went as she pleased. But Momma did not return home Saturday morning, which was a workday for her. This seemed perplexing, because she was both punctual and dependable, and—as best I can remember—had never missed a day of work or a Sunday service. Therefore, as morning approached noontime, I was overwrought with concern.

Saturday morning, about 9:00 a.m. her ride was on schedule to pick her up for work. The lady was out front honking the horn, and I did not have a clue about Momma's whereabouts. I felt the need to give an explanation but had none. Supposing her absence was some kind of fluke, to play it safe I made up a story to tell her. Knowing how prompt Momma was, the lady was also baffled. Still frightened but hopeful, I sat on one of the orange patio lounge chairs, watching and impatiently waiting for Momma to come home. Around noontime, my fear escalated, and my heart was deeply troubled.

I scrutinized each passing car and desperately hoped one would pull up in our driveway and Momma would get out. As I sat with my head hung down in despair, hours passed with no sign of her.

Suddenly, one of the neighbors came running towards me with a newspaper in her hand. Noticeably flustered, as she drew near, she asked, "Isn't this article about your mother?"

And it was. Momma was shot that Friday night and had been taken to a nearby hospital where she was pronounced dead on arrival. Although her identification was in her wallet, the hospital released information regarding her death to a local newspaper instead of notifying the family.

***

On top of dealing with her death, I had to also contend with the inconsiderate manner in which it had been handled. Screaming hysterically, I raced to the telephone to call my sister.

Shocked and in total disbelief, she bellowed, "No! No! That can't be true. Such information could not have possibly been released to the newspaper without the family first being notified."

What the newspaper had printed was true; my mother had, indeed, been killed. Some witnesses said that it was accidental. However, I have never learned the truth of what had actually happened that horrible and unforgettable night.

I am left with two unanswered questions. Who killed my mother? And why?

***

Life without Momma was never the same. Her death forced me to grow up in a very unkind world. As a battered wife, I did not have the luxury of properly grieving her death.

Poncho felt the loss of not having Momma around as much as I did, if not more. His persistent crying deepened my depression. (I was nearly on the verge of a breakdown myself.) Perhaps he thought that Momma would walk through the door and rescue him once again, as she had done so many times before. Other times I cried with him, as we clung to one another. However, despite our unendurable pain, life persisted.

Minutes seemed like hours, hours like days and days like weeks. Learning to take one day at a time came gradually but with great difficulty.

Eventually I got the hang of motherhood. I made every effort to be the mother to Poncho that Momma had been to us both. To add to my already bewildered life, I had another baby, who was also beautiful. And we named him Kelton Leonardo Hardwick.

Poncho happily welcomed his little brother to the family and was quite protective of him. We were all crammed into a tiny apartment with one bed, a crib for Kelton and a playpen that was converted into a bed at night for Poncho. Slowly but surely, I became more comfortable in my uncomfortable lifestyle. But I would soon know that my period of grieving was not yet over— by a long shot.

Eleven months after Momma's death, I suffered another painful and unforgettable blow. Poncho had spent the entire day with his fraternal grandmother. She brought him back home late that evening, around dinnertime, and we went about our normal routine. Poncho was seated in his highchair, and I placed his dinner in front of him.

Normally, he dove right into his dinner, but for some reason seemed more tired than usual. He was bubbly and energetic like most two-year-old boys. Therefore, I attributed his sluggishness to a long day out with his grandma.

Kelton was seated in my lap and I proceeded to feed him. But when I took Poncho out of his highchair, he had barely touched his food. After dinner I gave them both baths and put them to bed.

The next morning, Kelton had awakened bright eyed and full of life. After feeding and bathing him, I put toys in his crib so that he could play for a while.

Taking advantage of the fact that Poncho (who was my walking toddler) was still sleeping, I cleaned the apartment. When I peeped in on him, I thought to myself, *gosh, he must be really tired.* So I allowed him to sleep a bit longer.

Just a couple of hours before lunchtime, I walked over to the playpen to get him up for breakfast. I reached down into his bed and called out to him, "Poncho, Poncho, wake up baby. It's time for breakfast."

He offered no response.

"Come on! You have to wake up now sleepy head," I said nervously.

Still no response.

When I picked him up, his entire body went limp in my arms. It was then that I noticed the snorkeling, heavy sound of his breathing.

Extremely perplexed, I ran around the corner to my sister at work. Panting, I blurted, "You know Nita it's the oddest thing, Poncho is okay, I mean he is breathing. But I can't wake him up."

She immediately closed up the office, and we ran back to my apartment.

I was a bit unnerved by the alarming look in my sister's eyes when she saw Poncho. But when she said, "Laurette, this baby is sick," I completely fell apart emotionally.

We immediately rushed him to the hospital. The doctor thoroughly examined him, but could not readily diagnose the problem. Because my sister was older, the physician took her into his office to question her. He had hoped to find the antidote that would save my baby's life.

I sat alone at my baby's bedside, stroking his soft hair and pleading with him to wake up.

The night before, I started to braid his hair as I often did to keep his head cool on humid nights. When he collapsed on my lap, I lay him down with the intentions of finishing his hair the following morning. Little did I know that that would have been the last night I saw my baby alive.

I vividly remember thinking, *God this is just too much for a single human being to endure.*

The doctor instructed my sister and me to thoroughly search my apartment for medications or anything that Poncho could have possibly taken. My heart was pounding so fast; it felt as if it were literally being thrown against my chest. We turned my apartment upside down, but found absolutely nothing.

Meanwhile, I prayed that Poncho would still be alive when we returned to the hospital. But then, I really did not think it remotely possible that my little energetic boy could die.

After a thorough search, we empty-handedly rushed back to the hospital.

Grateful that he was still alive when we returned, I walked over to the window of his room to make a deal with God.

Please God save my baby's life, and I will ... But he never regained consciousness. I felt him dying.

Afraid of being alone when I was told the inevitable, I walked down the corridor to find my sister who was speaking with the doctor. An insensitive nurse said, "She doesn't even care". Apparently the nurse who spoke those almost unforgivable words had never lost someone whom she loved more than she loved herself.

Coming from the opposite direction, a lady approached me with opened arms. *Who she was or where she came from to this day I have no idea.* In her gentle, warm embrace I felt an inexpressible comfort. She then whispered softly in my ear, "I know you don't understand right now, but one day you will."

Drenching her shoulder with my tears, I sharply refuted, "I will never understand this. I prayed and God let me down."

And for many years after, I lamented over the deaths of my son and my mother.

Emotional pain from the loss of a loved one is not something easily dismissed. And never would I dare to suggest such a thing. But grieving is not supposed to consume an entire life, as it almost did mine.

For 30 years, I bemoaned the deaths of my mother and son. Many nights found me sleepwalking and crying out for them. Once while traveling by train, I jumped up and ran crying and screaming down the aisles. Thank God, I was with my dad, who quieted me with gentle restraint. But the entire scene left Dad befuddled, because he had never witnessed one of my episodes.

Other times I awakened in my kid's bed, not remembering how I got there. Once I was told that I sat up in the bed, patted the covers and cried, "Where's the baby? Where's the baby?"

Ultimately, grief and sadness consumed my life. It even overshadowed my love for God. And though I had forsaken Him, He never forsook me. As a Christian, I learned in Scripture that my obsessive and prolonged grieving was a form of idolatry. Anyone or anything we put before God, becomes our god. However, it took much counseling before I was able to completely overcome the worship of my idols. And yet God continued to be merciful and loving to me.

Later I gave birth to three other children. And God did many miraculous things for us, some of which I had no knowledge of at the time. One day, without my permission, and for something I would never have consented to, my children went swimming. Mike and Angie, who were only about 7 and 8 years old at the time, took my youngest son Curtis (C.J.), who was only 4 years old, to the neighborhood pool.

My three wanderers had gotten away from their eldest brother, Kelton, who was watching them while I was at work. C.J. has always possessed an abundance of confidence. And unattended on the pool deck, he jumped into six feet of water. The other kids were applauding, thinking that he was swimming. By God's grace, Michael realized that C.J. was drowning, jumped into the pool and saved him. They waited until they were young adults (way past the age for discipline) before they disclosed this heart-wrenching information to me.

Now young adults, my children revealed how they went swimming in lakes, along with many of their other life-endangering adventures. I listened, speechless, as they were cleansing their souls. Once I got past the initial shock of it all, with much appreciation and adoration I gave praise and thanks to God for protecting them. Some of the things God did for us, no human being could have done. God has wonderfully blessed my family, so much that it would take another book to tell it all.

God is good, and He has given us His only begotten Son, so that we may have eternal life. To quote my son, Curtis, "Everything else God does for us is a bonus."

It is a trick of the enemy to have us focus on our sufferings rather than glorifying God as Creator. The fact that we endure hardships in this sinful world does not make Him any less AWESOME. We are not to make gods out of people, as God is God ... all by Himself.

The day I overthrew my idols, those both living and those who have gone on to be with the Lord, my heart made room for God to set up residency where only He should dwell.

In order for us to heal, we must grieve—but not indefinitely. If you have spent an excessive amount of time worrying over situations and circumstances that you are powerless to change, it is time to move on. Protracted grief turns into idolatry. Satan would like nothing more than for us to blame God for permitting the deaths of our loved ones. In doing so, we alienate ourselves from God and open our hearts to idols.

Grieving is not idolatry. However, obsessing over someone or something is.

When we place anything or anyone before God, that individual or thing becomes our god. Not only is this applicable to the loss of a loved one from physical death; it also applies to the death of a relationship (such as divorce, alienation, or estrangement).

I spent most of my youth feeling victimized and sorry for myself. My mother and child were most definitely reigning on my heart's throne. Sadness, grief, and sorrow were my acquaintances and happiness seemed distant and unattainable. What is more, happiness is circumstantial and is subject to change.

But God's joy is everlasting.

***

Our earthly families are with us for a season, but God is with us always. Although I was blessed with earthly parents for guardianship, God is and always has been my Father. Momma died when I was seventeen and my father was away while I was growing up. But God has never left my side. He never leaves nor forsakes His children, despite our circumstances. Therefore, dethrone your idols, whatever or whomever it or they may be.

(Other idols may include money, spouse, self, children, jobs, health, an enemy or even a friend.)

Stop obsessively grieving and get busy executing God's plan for your life. Delight yourself in Him and He will give you the desires of your heart. Repent and Return to God and make Him your first love. For there is no Father but God and He alone is everlasting.

My Father knows best

*God is my Father,
and He knows what is best
I experience serenity
when I abide in His rest.*

*He soothes my sorrows,
and quiets all my fears,
He gives me His laughter
in exchange for my tears.*

*He gives me living waters,
for my unquenchable thirst
I have no other god before Him
my Father comes first.*

*Dethrone all your idols,
those both living and dead
And experience God's peace
to the utmost instead.*

Children are God's Heritage

Naive and reticent, I was impregnated at the age of sixteen. And like countless other teenage girls, I was amateurishly embarking on motherhood. According to Robert T. Brown M.D., *"Every year almost one million teenage girls become pregnant and more than half of them are 17 years of age or younger when they have their first pregnancy."*

Teenage pregnancy is an epidemic that has no respect of a young girl's ethnicity, religion, or financial status. However, girls who are either impoverished, or have strong morals due to their upbringing or religious beliefs, are more inclined to carry their baby full term and give birth. Many others resort to abortions or have miscarriages.

At first glance, it would appear that the average teenage girl is an incurable romantic. But in reality her guise of romanticism, no doubt, is indicative of a co-dependent in the making. After indulging in heart-throbbing novels and romance movies, she pursues a love that generally exists only in her fantasies. Starry eyed with cupid's bow in hand, she gallivants around town as a predator in pursuit of love, but usually becomes the prey. Traveling light, the only thing she carries in her baggage is a hollow and empty heart. And alas! Cupid's arrow will not penetrate the heart of her hunted prey, because his own pursuit is merely that of a one-night stand.

After predator meets prey, they spend an enchanting night of magic and romance. At dawn, the stirring of harsh reality lurks at her bedside. Abruptly she awakens, only to find her hunted prey is not the true love that she desperately sought, but a counterfeit. And to add insult to her emotional injury, she later learns that she has also conceived.

Overwhelmingly distraught by her pregnancy and oblivious to motherhood, she fears the inevitable. In all probability, she will be a single parent, rearing her child alone.

This scenario has transpired throughout the ages of time. But it is more common now. It has often been said that opposites attract, but there is nothing more magnetic than two emotionally dejected people are.

Like a 747 lifting off the ground with insufficient fuel, their relationship has no where to go but down. To make matters worse, this couple has now brought a child into their insufferable world. Although both of them lack emotional sustenance, the girl is often portrayed as the victim of abandonment. But in truth, she is often equally responsible for severing the relationship.

Most teenage girls find it difficult to believe that they are worthy to be loved. And fear of abandonment often causes them to terminate their relationships—via sabotage. After all, if she forces him to leave, it's far better than him walking out on her.

All the same, whether she pushes him away or he leaves on his own, an innocent child will most likely suffer pain and rejection. Children born to these couples are epidemically suffering by the masses. Approximately three million children are either abused or witness abuse of domestic violence in their homes, which is equally devastating.

Furthermore, while they are loaned to their parents for a season, children actually belong to God. Parents are merely stewards over God's children to help shape them during their formative years. Many parents inadvertently think children are their own possessions. But the dangers of misunderstanding a child's purpose often result in child abuse. Given that such parents seem to give themselves permission to maltreat the children.

Often I have heard folk say, "If you mess with my child, you mess with me." Likewise, If you mess with God's children, you mess with Him.

In Matthew 18:2-6 the Bible states, "And He called a little child to Himself and put him in the midst of them. And said, Truly I say to you, unless you repent (change, turn about) and become like little children [trusting, lowly, loving, forgiving], you can never enter the kingdom of heaven [at all]. Whoever will humble himself therefore and become like this little child [trusting, lowly, loving, forgiving] is greatest in the kingdom of heaven. And whoever receives and accepts and welcomes one little child like this for My sake and in My name receives and accepts and welcomes Me. But whoever causes one of these little ones who believe in and acknowledge and cleave to Me to stumble and sin [that is, who entices him or hinders him in right conduct or thought], it would be better (more expedient and profitable or advantageous) for him to have a great millstone fastened around his neck and to be sunk in the depth of the sea."

God highly regards His people, especially His little ones. Therefore, no parent should be a stumbling block to a child's mental, emotional, or spiritual growth. It is a fact that God suffers long with us, but the abuse of a child saddens Him.

Stewardship is a privilege, and if you have been blessed with it, be faithful. After all, children are not our property to do with as we please. When their spirits are broken, God's ears are open to their cries, as He is both omniscient and omnipresent. He is everywhere, sees all, and is all knowing. Hebrews 4:13 says, "And not a creature exists that is concealed from His sight, but all things are open and exposed, naked and defenseless to the eyes of Him with Whom we have to do."

Whether loud and bodacious or soft and subtle, demeaning words cut like a knife to the core of a child's emotions. Also, when vulgarities are spewed out at them, God hears. Or when a child is sexually violated and physically abused, God sees.

Verbal and physical abuse devastates and emotionally cripples its victim. Furthermore, it strips them of their self-confidence and self-worth. Some children may spend their entire lives emotionally crippled as a result of the abuse they suffered during their formative years. Abused children may experience difficulty as adults loving themselves and being loved by others. Generally, with the exception of the few who get counseling and receive restoration, abused and neglected children grow up to be abusive parents.

All parents, myself included, have missed the mark during child rearing. Imperfect people can not be perfect parents. Still, deliberate abuse is not pleasing to God. Although the mistakes I made were unintentional, my children's lives were still negatively impacted.

Children are to be lovingly disciplined for their good, not punished and abused out of anger, shame, or resentment to satisfy the parent's frustration. Their childhood years should be safe and secure.

It is of the utmost importance for them to be able to trust their parents. For that reason, abusive parents must seek God's remedial help to refrain from any further abuse to their children.

In the Old Testament times, God was frequently referred to by His many names (which are descriptive of His character). Three of His names come to mind in this particular instance. The first name is "Jehovah Rapha", which informs that the Lord will heal you emotionally, physically, and spiritually (Exodus 15:26). Subsequent to experiencing His healing power, you may also as a whole individual come to know Him as "Jehovah Shalom" (Judges 6:24), which means peace in right relationship with God and man (i.e., your children). Additionally, after being a recipient of God's healing and peace, you may then know Him as "Jehovah Rohi, " our loving Father, Who protects, provides, and guides us (Psalm 23-1).

***

Over time, I came to know God as my healer, comforter, and provider. And after receiving His forgiveness and comfort, I was able to forgive myself. Equal to the task of forgiving myself, I had to admit my wrong doings and seek the forgiveness of the young adults whom I had reared. I also learned that being the parent did not automatically make me right. I needed to listen and respect my children's opinions as well when they expressed themselves. Although the parent is not always right, parenthood is a position of authority and should be respected. Respect should be reciprocal, but is not always done enthusiastically. Parents must both earn and encourage respect.

Humbling and healing work together, but pride will devour both. When we need to make a bad situation right, we must first be willing to admit that we were wrong. This may be difficult for parents who have spent years trying to convince our children that we know it all.

Children are a lot wiser than we credit them, and they often know when we are wrong. Besides, there is nothing more heroic than humbly asking a child's forgiveness. We must forgive ourselves as well. Henry Ward Beecher said, *"I can forgive, but I cannot forget," is only another way of saying, "I will not forgive." Forgiveness ought to be like a cancelled note — torn in two, and burned up, so that it never can be shown against one.*

God is willing to forgive and more than able to guide you through the process of parenting. If God can forgive you, why can't you forgive yourself? While repentance is the greatest gift that we can give to God, forgiveness is the greatest gift that we can give to ourselves.

To repent means to turn away from your sins (i.e., the abuse of your children), and return to God. But please let it be duly noted, "Children are God's Heritage."

Psalm 127:3 - Behold, children are a heritage from the Lord, the fruit of the womb a reward.

Children are God's Heritage

Children are sent from heaven
but only for a season,
And God has chosen parents,
solely for His reason

Their lives must be secure,
so shower them with love
And this will be well pleasing
to their Father up above

As stewards of the Lord,
we must not do them harm,
For when their cries go before Him,
it sends off an alarm

To parents who are abusive,
it's time that you relent
Before God and His children,
on bended knee repent.

No Greater Love

A mother's love for her child runs the length of the Nile River. It is as deep as the Pacific Ocean, and stands as tall as Mount Everest. Her love knows no boundaries, has no limitations, and comes second to none but God's love. This unconditional love allows mothers to be representatives of God. In most cases, a fetus is securely wrapped in his mother's love from the moment (s)he enters her womb. And she experiences heartfelt joy with the mere movement of her baby.

Prior to the birth of her baby, a mother painstakingly searches for the perfect name. And when her baby arrives, her insufferable childbearing pangs are replaced with indescribable joy. In the same manner that a lioness protects her cub, these mothers will protect their young by any means necessary.

A mother-child relationship consists of giving and receiving through many stages as the child's needs change. Even as a fetus, nourishment is provided through the mother's umbilical cord and after birth from her breast or a bottle. With the security and comfort of the mother's love, her baby continues to grow.

Before very long, the child passes through adolescence on their journey toward adulthood. And, while, the child's notable physical change is graspable, their emotional transformation is somewhat mystifying. Like a sucker punch, a mother is more than slightly unprepared for her child's independence and individuality. In my opinion, and based upon personal observations, these often prove to be the most emotional challenging and perplexing times in a mother's life. Suddenly, her endearing child, whom she has so deeply loved through the years, has grown up and is barely recognizable.

Most mothers spend half their lifetime investing love deposits into the emotional bank of their children, later to find them lacking in sufficient love for their moms when we desire to make a withdrawal.

A number of adult children are either unwilling or incapable of loving their parents selflessly. Their rejection causes parents (usually their mother), crushing emotional pain. Similarly, we experience a perfect love from God, and yet we falter in our love towards Him. In fact, the reason that we can love our children as deeply and unconditionally is because God has placed this love within us. Our love for them will overall be stronger than their love for us.

When we truly understand our purpose, and come to terms with our role as a parent, the task will be less burdensome and more pleasurable. A substantial amount of our pain comes from a sense of responsibility for the negative decisions that our offspring make as young adults. Our guilt is compounded when we witness them suffering the consequences of their decisions.

Despite the love and nurturing of many parents, some children are wayward and go astray. Parents who have given their children a healthy and wholesome upbringing should in no way blame themselves or feel responsible for their adult children's actions. And for those of us who have made countless mistakes, we must also realize that our young adults must be held responsible for their own choices. For peace of mind, and to avoid setting ourselves up for disappointment, we must discard any unrealistic expectations of them or ourselves. Removing our expectations will alleviate much of our pain.

While, some adult children are respectful, many others are purposely disrespectful. I strongly suggest that blatant disrespect not be tolerated. When a young adult is persistent in displaying an attitude of disrespect, parents might consider disengaging from the relationship until respect is reinstated. They must be challenged to change any and all such behaviors. Ogden Nash, the late author and poet of children's books said,

> *"Children aren't happy*
> *with nothing to ignore,*
> *and that's what parents*
> *were created for."*

Furthermore, it is important for mother and adult child to detach in a timely manner. This prevents a prolonged unhealthy attachment of mutual dependency. Thereby, causing the adult child to become stagnant, disabling their mental and emotional growth. Try to visualize an adult wearing diapers and drinking from a baby bottle. As bizarre as that sounds, it is not much different from a young adult who is still dependent upon and emotionally attached to their parents.

Abnormal attachments will almost certainly lead to a strain on inter-reliant ties. The third chapter of Ecclesiastes says, "To everything there is a season, and a time for every matter or purpose under heaven: "A time to cast away stones and a time to gather, a time to embrace and a time to refrain from embracing, a time to get and a time to lose, a time to keep and a time to cast away, a time to rend and a time to sew, a time to keep silent and a time to speak." And verse eleven states, "He has made everything beautiful in its time."

A twenty-year-old, would look very odd nursing his mother's breast for milk, and so would a 30 year old who was still potty training.

Many adult children ranging anywhere from the ages of 25 to 40 (and in some cases, even older) are experiencing the *revolving door syndrome*. They return to their parent's home for shelter and refuse to take full responsibility for their own lives. Although extenuating circumstances could create this situation, these adult children may be unable to function on their own. Crippled, no doubt, by their co-dependencies(in most cases) with their mothers.

Many parents enter into parenthood inexperienced and emotionally maimed. Without essential parenting skills, rearing a child is like running a marathon with a broken leg; we most likely will not win, but are rushed off our feet with guilt when we lose.

The guilt that drives us to compensate for our past mistakes commonly results in our overcompensating. This often proves to be equally detrimental to the child's emotional health. Overindulged children usually grow up to be selfish and dependent adults. Some children were not properly taught, because their parents had an emotional deficiency and could not adequately teach them. Besides, what has been done in the past, cannot be undone or redone.

Every fruit-bearing tree brings forth fruit of its own kind. Apples grow from apple trees, oranges from orange trees, and bananas from banana trees. Trees with healthy roots produce healthy fruit; likewise, trees with unhealthy roots produce spoiled fruit. Similarly, women who are emotionally damaged will most likely rear emotionally unhealthy children. Nevertheless, at the age of accountability, all that the adult child has not received from their parents, (s)he is responsible to seek from God.

Although we as parents have often failed our children, God will not. At any rate, it is pointless to continue the unproductive cycle of mutual dependency that will inevitably lead to nowhere. We are not capable of changing the past. But with restoration, we can make better choices in the future.

Having a different mental picture of the adult children is helpful when severing co-dependent ties. Therefore, instead of continually calling them my children, I refer to them as the young adults that I have reared. Which first of all helped me to envision them as separate functioning individuals. And secondly, eliminating the word *my* (a possessive adjective), helps me to remember that they belong to God. Also, while praying, I visualize myself standing before God and placing them into His capable hands.

This process of recovery is one of trial and error, but each step taken is more liberating than the previous one. Once the pathway to emotional freedom is embarked upon, it must be maintained throughout life.

A Different Love

*As children travel,
from womb to breast
In their mother's love,
they know they'll find rest.*

*A mother's love
is from heaven's domain,
She loves and forgives them,
again and again.*

*Around her young ones,
the sun rises and sets,
And although she's forgotten,
she never forgets.*

*When her heart is filled with pain,
and aches to the core,
This different kind of love
will make room for much more.*

Victim of Rape

According to the U.S. Department of Justice, somewhere in America a woman is raped every 2 minutes.

Dispirited women are overcome with shame and guilt, when their rapist dominates their bodies. Not only are the victim's bodies intruded upon, but their minds and emotions as well. Most rape victims believe that they were in some way responsible. But contrary to this belief; the deranged and distorted sickness of rapists motivates them to commit such a malicious and deplorable crime of hate and control.

***

One evening I had planned a surprise party for a friend - nothing elaborate, just some ice cream and a birthday cake. When my friend did not show up, my kids and I happily indulged in the birthday goodies. Immediately after, we took our baths and prepared for bed.

Our house rule was to securely lock all doors and windows at bedtime. And for extra precaution, I had a deadbolt lock put on the front door. In addition, I jammed the glass sliding door shut with a stick.

The kids retired to their bedroom, and my toddler snuggled up next to me under a warm comforter. Before long we were all fast asleep.

I was awakened by the awareness of a presence in my bedroom. At first, I was somewhat calm and assumed that one of my kids was restless and wanted to climb in my bed. But none of their voices called out to me, and the silence was very cold and eerie.

Knowing that I was not alone interrupted my slow drift back into sleep. Finally, after a momentary struggle I was able to lift my heavy eyelids, only to find that my vision was obscured by the thick darkness. I distinctly remember that night being terribly unkind; not even a sliver of light entered the bedroom.

As my eyes adjusted to the darkness, I detected the silhouette of a man. Although I was unable to see him clearly, I did get a glimpse of a shiny object in his hand. By then I was wide-awake and panic stricken beyond words. Not only had sleep fled, but also it would be several months after that horrible night before it returned to me again.

Petrified, I nervously asked, "What do want? Why are you in my apartment?"

His momentary silence was as frightening as his presence.

Suddenly, I felt the piercing tip of his knife pressed into my face as he whispered revolting obscenities. Breathing heavily, he warned me to be quiet or else.

I had often thought about what I would do if I were attacked. Deep down inside, I never thought that it would ever happen to me. I thought that victims of rape were people who were the subject of news reports on television or in the papers. All the same, like many women, I still contemplated preventative strategies, just in case.

I thought that I would defend myself by any means necessary. Perhaps I would kick the rapist in his groin or strike him with a heavy object. Even pepper mace seemed an option, which I never bothered to purchase. And in hopes that the assailant would spare my life, *plan b* was to surrender to him and get it over with as quickly as possible.

When attacked, I abandoned both plans and screamed hysterically, "Help! Help! Help! Please somebody, help me please!"

Minutes seemed like hours as I continued to scream frantically for help. The thought of a grimy stranger raping me was not only repugnant; at the time it seemed a fate worse than death. Determined to rape me, my merciless aggressor beat my face as though it was a punching bag. And I, equally determined not to let him, gripped my gown tightly together with both hands. After wrestling me to the floor, he sliced through the tips of my fingers with his knife to free my nightgown. Before long, my mint green gown was stained with blood.

Where are my neighbors and my babysitter? I frightfully thought to myself. And as I waited for what seemed an eternity, any hope of being helped gradually began to dwindle.

Suddenly my bedroom door opened and my nine-year-old son stood in the doorway. At first I was relieved, but seeing the intruder run towards him with a knife was by far the most fearsome moment of that entire evening. Scared stiff, I immediately jumped to my feet and was prepared to fight for my boy ... although just moments earlier, I was too afraid to attempt to save my own life. But, thank God, the rapist ran past my son and existed through the same window, which he had apparently made his entrance.

***

When the attacker left, I managed to unlock the front door and raced over to my neighbor's apartment. Banging desperately on her bedroom window, I pleaded for her help. She came over, helped us get situated and called 911.

The policemen arrived and found me traumatized, bruised, and bloody. The officers took pictures and made out their report. They took me down to the station to view mug shots.

Regrettably, I was unable to make a positive identification or give any description of the rapist. Still, I was determined to put him behind bars, and went down to the station daily. The officers grew weary of my continual visits, but I felt at risk knowing that the perpetrator was roaming free.

***

Rape is an age-old crime. Victims of rape often blame themselves for the atrocious crime against them. I often wondered did my attire attract the rapist. *Was it the way I walked or talked? What would make someone attack me so brutally?* Other rape victims often ponder my questions, as well.

Even the women of biblical times who dressed modestly were raped. Such was the case in the book of Deuteronomy 22:25-27: "But if a man finds the betrothed maiden in the open country and the man seizes her and lies with her, then only the man who lay with her shall die. But you shall do nothing to the young woman: she has committed no sin punishable by death, for this is as when a man attacks and slays his neighbor. For he came upon her in the open country and the betrothed girl cried out, but there was no one to save her."

The Bible clearly states that rape was not the victim's fault.

In the book of Ruth, Boaz admonished Ruth to stay close to his young maidens for her protection until they harvested the entire crop. And Naomi, her mother-in-law, warned her to be careful of being molested. The young maidens were often raped when they went into the fields to glean. Ruth 2:8-9 states: Then Boaz said to Ruth, "Listen my daughter, do not go to glean in another field or leave this one, but stay here close by my maidens. Watch which field they reap, and follow them. Have I not charged the young men not to molest you?"

***

God ordained sexual relations exclusively for married

couples. It is not His will for anyone to be sexually assaulted and violated. Rape is a non-consensus act. In the Old Testament times, men were actually put to death for committing sexual crimes.

II Samuel, chapter 13 records molestation and rape among siblings and other family members. King David was devastated when he learned that his son Amnon had raped his half sister, Tamar.

Amnon's desire for Tamar was so strong that he became physically ill. His crafty friend Jonadab advised him on how to deviously get his sister into his bed. Amnon deceived their father, King David, by requesting to have the girl bring him food. Verse 10, states, "Then Amnon said to Tamar, Bring the food here into the bedroom, so I may eat from your hand.

So Tamar took the cakes she had made and brought them into the room to Amnon her brother. And when she brought them to him he took hold of her and said, Come lie with me, my sister.

She replied, No my brother! Do not force and humble me, for no such thing should be done in Israel! Do not do this foolhardy, scandalous thing! And I, how could I rid myself of my shame? And you, you will be [considered] one of the stupid fools in Israel. Now therefore, I pray you, speak to the king, for he will not withhold me from you."

Apparently, if Amnon had asked their father, King David, for permission, he would have permitted him to marry his half-sister. But as with all rapists, Amnon did not love Tamar.

He merely lusted after her, and against her will, he raped her.

Finally, in verses, 14-15, " But he would not listen to her, and being stronger than she, he forced her and lay with her. Then Amnon hated her exceedingly, so that his hatred for her was greater than the love with which he had loved her. And Amnon said to her, Get up and get out!" Tamar was deeply ashamed and felt much despair because of the way her brother had treated her.

***

Rape is insufferable, and doubtless one of the most appalling ordeals its victim will suffer. Nevertheless, victims of rape should not allow themselves to be overcome with shame, blame, or guilt, thereby self-inflicting further emotional pain.

The rape victim should avoid isolating herself. She is not the guilty party. If anyone needs to hide let the rapist go crawl in a hole.

***

The good news is that even when your life has been scarred by a sexual crime, healing is available. And remember you are not alone. Seek counseling from a support group. Counseling promotes healing. Moreover, as victims, we owe it to ourselves and to society to make the rapist accountable for their actions, which may prevent them from committing further acts of crime.

Forgiveness is spoken of repeatedly in this book. It is essential that we forgive, as forgiveness is the key that sets us free. While forgiveness may or may not be beneficial to the victimizer, it is always beneficial to the victim. Internalized anger may cause the victim to suffer emotionally, mentally, and physically. Although my attacker did not sexually assault me, I was physically and emotionally traumatized. The devastation of that night may scar my children and me for the rest of our lives. But instead of allowing myself to be defeated, I chose to be a survivor.

***

God faithfully honored His promise to give me beauty for the ashes of my life.

Got ashes? Give them to God. He is a restorer of those who have been emotionally and mentally wounded. A willingness to forgive is a major step towards your healing process. And God, who is Sovereign, is only a prayer away.

Women of Rape

Our bodies belong to us,
A God's given treasure,
Divinely formed,
for our husband's good pleasure.

Prohibited to strangers,
lurking during the night,
And forbidden to perverts,
scurrying during daylight.

Although our bodies are fragile,
of soft and gentle form,
Our God-given strength within
could weather any storm.

We've taken life's best blows;
still we spring back to our feet
You brush pass us quite often
while walking down the street.

Heart Behind Prison Bars

One night, I had an awful dream that I will always remember. The dream was that before long my son, Michael, was going to be incarcerated.

What a nightmare that was. Just the mere thought of him being behind prison bars had me shaking and frantic with fear.

When I had awakened the next morning, my hair was matted to my head with sweat and tears. Totally a basket case and unable to function, I called in to inform my employer that I would not be in to work that day.

I called Tom, a good friend. He was a member of the church that we attended and a devout Christian. He came to my house and we talked at length about my concerns regarding my son. He had a long heart-to-heart talk with Michael, as well. Tom was truly a blessing to us that day. Before he left, he prayed with us. By then my spirits were lifted and I had calmed down considerably.

Perhaps it sounds a bit strange that I was so unnerved by a mere dream. However, the dream seemed all too real. Some time ago, I even prayed to die and go to heaven rather than living and seeing my children endure hardships in life. Now, how bazaar is that? Thank God, He knows which of our prayers to answer and which ones to ignore.

The devastation that I experienced while growing up, had me petrified of what they may possibly have to endure.

***

Over the years, I taught my children what I knew about emotional healing to cushion their journey through life. I had hoped that life would be a whole lot easier for them than it was for me. But life often takes a different course than we plan; and sometimes despite our best efforts, bad things happen. Yet, God is faithful to see us through it all.

***

Over time, the nightmare became a depressing reality when a policeman who posed as a friendly neighborhood officer visited our home. (In retrospect, I understand that he was only doing his job, but his techniques were unethical.) He actually took my son out of my hands, like an adult would take candy from a child.

We lived in an upper class poor neighborhood - not quite gutter, but the nearest thing to it. When you are impoverished and without knowledge of your legal rights, having an officer in your home can be somewhat intimidating. I felt so manipulated by him.

After spending time with us and gaining our confidence, the man then asked if he could take my son down to the police station for further questioning. I agreed, only because I was so afraid that if I did not, later he might have harassed my son.

Michael, who was merely a minor at the time, did not have legal representation and was not read his rights. And neither one of us were informed that we had the option to refuse the detective's request. Although Michael was around fourteen years of age, they treated him as an adult down at the station.

Several long and stressful hours had passed, and I sat impatiently waiting for my son to be brought home, paralyzed with fear. All of my nerves were pivoting in the pit of my stomach.

I believe that many law enforcers manipulate people who are financially challenged and without knowledge of their legal rights.

After hours of interrogation by the officer, Michael informed him of some trouble he had gotten into previously. Without notifying me, the imposter hauled my son off to the detention center, where he was detained.

Crime should not go unpunished, I am not suggesting that; nor had I ever given my son that impression. Nonetheless, people do have legal rights and are entitled to them.

***

One day I went to the courthouse to plead with the judge on behalf of my son. Fear-stricken, I trembled outside her chambers. The letter that I had written was clinched tightly in the palm of my sweaty hand. Actually, a fair hearing and some type of restorative counseling were all that I wanted for him.

I will always be eternally grateful to the judge. She greeted me warmly, refused the letter and invited me into her chambers instead. She gave me her undivided attention while I nervously expressed myself on my son's behalf. The judge's compassion was exactly what I needed to get me through that nail-biting day.

Michael was in an identity crisis and a sure candidate to succumb to peer pressure as he grew up striving determinedly for acceptance. He often went out exploring the yard for old empty bottles and wildflowers (weeds). After making his version of a floral arrangement, he raced home to surprise me.

My heart was overwhelmed time and again as I looked into Michael's big bright eyes - his face covered with sand. Of all my children, Michael had the darkest complexion and the fullest features. These qualities make him a strikingly handsome man. But back then, he was often teased and rejected by some of the other kids.

Mrs. Haler, his second grade teacher, took an interest in him. "I wish that I could always be Michael's teacher," she said, "because I fear he will often be misunderstood."

I too, feared that Michael would be misunderstood. But never once had I considered that his behavior caused people to reject him. I realize now that he was in a no-win situation. He often misbehaved to get attention, but as a result got negative attention instead.

Michael's persistence for getting into trouble eventually sent him to prison. And I was emotionally shipwrecked.

Some mornings, I woke up so hopelessly depressed that getting out of bed was a major task. Other days would find me feeling extremely angry, helpless, and betrayed by the penal system.

Nights were much more difficult to endure. I often spent them awake, fearful, and worrying. Swept away with guilt and grief, I blamed myself for Michael's actions.

My son and I were both serving a prison term. While he was behind bars physically, my heart was behind prison's bars emotionally. There were many times I was unavailable for my other family members, including my husband. I was physically present with my family, but emotionally incarcerated with Michael.

Plagued by a guilty conscience, I felt that I had no right to be happy while he was suffering. Taunting voices in my head persisted, *had you raised him properly he would not be incarcerated.* While my son was suffering, I had determined that I was going to suffer along with him.

Later, I came to realize that my reasoning was obscured by my own warped emotions. I had spent a great deal of time over the years attempting to rescue Michael, which I later learned benefited neither one of us. I allowed myself to suffer emotionally for the wrong choices that he made.

I reared my children as best I could, which was far from perfect, considering my emotional state at the time. Nevertheless, I gave all that I had to give. I instilled Biblical principles in them. They were loved, fed, clothed, and sheltered.

***

Implementing strong family values, nurturing, and a healthy form of discipline may certainly help to shape children. However, growing up in a dysfunctional home has caused some parents to lack these essential parenting skills.

Furthermore, parents will without doubt make mistakes while rearing their children. Also, more restorative programs for rehabilitation can certainly improve the penal system, and possibly cut down on tax dollars spent to house habitual offenders.

Adult children are responsible for their own actions, and they must be allowed to live their own lives. As parents, most of us have learned from our many mistakes—life is a learning experience for our children, as well.

Get out of unrest and into God's rest. Initially it may be difficult to stop obsessively worrying, simply because it's a familiar tendency.

The transition from worry to rest starts with making the decision to cast our cares upon the Lord. Proverbs 3:5-6 (amplified) "Lean on, trusts in, and be confident in the Lord with all your heart and mind and do not rely on your own insight or understanding. In all your ways know, recognize, and acknowledge Him and He will direct and make straight and plain your paths."

***

With a clearer spiritual and emotional awareness, I have learned to trust God with the young adults whom I have reared for Him. The Bible states that whom the Lord loves, He chastens and does not destroy. Allow your young adults to be responsible for their own actions. And forgive yourself.

As mothers, guilt weighs heavily upon our hearts, which is why it is so important that we learn to forgive ourselves. Mom, why are you serving prison time for someone else's crime?

Get involved in a prayer group at your church. If you are not a member of a church, find one that is teaching sound doctrine and that has wholesome fellowship.

There is much hope and comfort in the word of God. Read your Bible. Pray and ask God to strengthen you. And instead of wasting precious time being overcome with guilt, put time to better use by becoming an intercessory prayer warrior for your loved ones.

Resume your life by putting one foot in front of the other. And remember, with God all things are possible.

Open the prison door

*I spent much time
behind prison doors,
All stretched out
on its cold, hard floors.*

*I spent much time,
climbing a prison wall,
Marching up and down
in the prison's hall.*

*I spent much time
staring at the prison's ceiling,
Eating prison food,
while having a nauseating feeling.*

*I spent much time in prison,
for a crime I had no part,
I was not there in body,
but in mind, emotions and heart.*

Grandchildren

Grandchildren are wonderful bundles of bliss. They bring unspeakable joy and happiness into the lives of their grandparents. Hearing the sweet voices of my grandchildren uttering the name Grandma fills my heart with inexpressible joy. And in many cases, we as grandmothers share a bond with our grandchild that is perhaps stronger than the one we shared with our adult children, during their childhood. I enjoy such a bonding with my grandchildren, because I am wiser and more stable than I was as a younger woman.

Grandchildren are cherished and very endearing to their grandmothers. But their purpose for being in our lives is often misconstrued. We adore them. Yet in a subtle and non-suspecting way, we believe that the purpose of our grandchildren is to make amends for the voluminous mistakes we made while rearing our children. And now, as we observe our young adults making bad choices and mistakes in rearing their children, as grandmothers we have the tendency to feel responsible—indirectly.

Women who are inundated with guilt about past failures during child rearing are more susceptible to (what I call) the *intrusive grandmother syndrome (I.G.S.)*: the obsession of re-parenting our adult children on how to rear their children.

The parent's credibility may be diminished in their children's eyes as a result of I.G.S. Such interference often sends mixed messages to the grandchildren. Many of them find it difficult to comprehend whether the parent or the grandparent is the primary authoritative figure.

My grandson, Laurence, often complained to me about things his mother did that displeased him, and I encouraged him to express his discontent. I assured him that I would confront his mother about his displeasures. I gave Laurence the impression that I was parenting both him and his mother. What's more, I once saw a tee shirt that read "If momma says no call 1(800) grandma."

***

After speaking to many women with similar life experiences, I have concluded such dependency is more prevalent among mothers, adult daughters and their daughter's children. Many adult children will strongly resent the interference of (*I.G.S.*), while others may welcome it for their own gain. But with all intents and purposes, such meddling only has a tendency towards emotional devastation. As all persons involved will be affected by it. An unhealthy tie between mother and adult child will most likely snowball, extending to yet another generation — the grandchild.

There was an influential and uncanny parallel in the relationships between my mother, my daughter and myself. Counseling enlightened me on how deeply it had impacted my life.

Typically, daughters impersonate their mother's negative behavior patterns. That, along with my personal life's traumas, redoubled my instability.

My daughter, Angela, and I were both about the same age when we gave birth to our first-borns, which were boys.

I was a teenager. My mother took me to all my doctor's appointments; for the same reason, I took my daughter to all of hers. During the birth of my son, my mother was with me the entire time. And from the hospital we moved in with Momma—she parented the both of us. Following the same pattern, my daughter and grandson lived with me — I parented both of them. In the span of one year, I lost my mother and my first-born son to death. Although both were extremely traumatic, my son's death left me bound by a misguided sense of guilt. Time after time, I relived that day, wondering if perhaps I had missed something. *What could I have possibly done that may have saved his life?*

When my daughter was born, both my mother and first-born son had already been deceased for about seven years. But the learned behavior of my mother was alive and well within me. And because I had not properly dealt with the pain and guilt after their deaths (especially my baby), the dependency between my daughter, my grandson, and myself was heightened.

Emotionally, I stepped into my mother's shoes, and my daughter (as far as I was concerned) had stepped into mine. My daughter's life was similar to my own, which caused my dormant pain to gradually resurface. During this extremely perplexing time, I was incapable of emotionally differentiating my deceased son from my grandson, Laurence.

In the midst of my madness, unintentionally I trampled over my daughter's emotions. And nothing she did as it pertained to Laurence was ever good enough for me. As an over-protective grandmother, I appointed myself as a round-the-clock advisor to prevent her from going through what I had gone through. But my methods to spare my daughter from pain caused her greater pain. The underlying force that drove me to save my grandson was the need to save my own son, whom I had already lost.

Guilt drove me out of control. I was my own worst enemy. The agitating thorn of my soul was guilt and selfishness. I bounced back and forth emotionally from self-blame to self-condemnation. At other times I simply submerged myself in self-pity over my son's death. My real problem was that I had become way too self-indulged.

The obsession I had with Laurence seemed to overshadow my love for the other grandchildren. Although I loved them all equally, at times my actions depicted otherwise. Overtime, the distress that I was causing the others only increased my preexisting anguish and guilt.

Wisdom attained over years leads many grandmothers to believe they are more qualified to rear their grandchildren than are their parents. But despite what we may believe, our grandchildren's mindsets (along with the times) have changed considerably.

And since our adult children are more familiar with their children's generation, in most cases, they are better able to deal with the situations their children face daily.

As grandparents, we play a significant role in the lives of our grandchildren. We are to impart wisdom and Biblical truths to them, and assist in teaching them to grow up to be morally upstanding adults. But their upbringing is the sole responsibility of their parents.

We must be cognizant of not overstepping the boundaries our adult children set for their children. There are some valid reasons for grandmothers to rear their grandchildren (such as in the case of an emergency, illness, or death). But guilt and making amends for past mistakes are not valid reasons.

Guilty hearts have caused countless of us to give up our lives and our dreams. And many have forsaken roles as grandmothers to become mothers to their grandchildren. They forfeit most of their lives in an attempt to live someone else's (i.e., their adult children).

Benjamin Franklin said of life, *"Were it offered to my choice, I should have no objection to a repetition of the same life from its beginning, only asking the advantages authors have in a second edition to correct some faults in the first"*

Women who spend the better part of their lives tormented by the past cheat themselves out of the wonderful opportunity of embracing their golden years.

It is imperative to understand that no amount of guilt or agonizing over the past is going to change one iota of it. As grandmothers, we do ourselves a grave injustice when we harshly judge ourselves. After all, had we known yesterday what we know today, we would have been spared some mistakes. On the other hand, we would be void of wisdom attained by mistakes made in the school of life. Furthermore, our damaged emotions are an inheritance from many generations ago. We (no disrespect intended) were involuntarily born into the sinful lineage of our forefathers.

Genesis, the third chapter, elaborates on the serpent's rebellious plan against God to bring corruption into the awe-inspiring paradise called "The Garden of Eden". God prepared it for Adam, who later shared it with his wife, Eve. God's one stipulation in the beautiful garden was to not eat of the forbidden tree.

But the serpent, who was cunning and crafty, beguiled Eve. And Eve, having been manipulated by the serpent, did eat of the tree. She then enticed Adam to eat, thereby disobeying a direct command from God.

It was then sin entered the world, instigating our damaged emotions.

***

Therefore, release yourself from the shackles of guilt. It took much prayer and counseling to help me get to the root of my dormant pain. Wise counsel, love, and the patience of Job that my husband gave me helped me enormously.

After being set free, I offered a sincere apology to my adult children and commenced to sever all unhealthy ties.

When your adult children make mistakes while rearing their children, don't blame yourself. Do not abandon them altogether, but prayerfully learn your place and get in it.

While grandmothers should be available if needed, we must also discern if the need is valid. Be mindful not to revert to familiar patterns of *the intrusive grandmother syndrome (I.G.S.)*.

Reclaim your life!

During the course of my recovery, I read many books and listened to numerous tapes, but one of the greatest sources of help I received through God, was from Willie, my husband, counselor, and best friend.

Grandchildren

Grandchildren are like jewels
they're as precious as a gem.
We're to warm them with our love,
and forever cherish them.

Their visits should be special,
but they do not come to stay
Give them hugs, milk, and cookies
then send them on their way.

Enjoy the golden years of life,
for you there is no other
Leave the rearing of your grands,
to their father and their mother.

A Stepmother's Woes

The role of a stepmother is a journey many women travel, only to find the road paved with grief, difficulty, and great challenge. One of the Biblical references to a stepmother is found in Genesis 16:1-6: "Now Sarai, Abram's wife, had borne him no children. She had an Egyptian maid whose name was Hagar. And Sarai said to Abram, See here, the Lord has restrained me from bearing [children]. I am asking you to have intercourse with my maid; it may be that I can obtain children by her. And Abram listened and heeded to what Sarai said.

So Sarai, Abram's wife, took Hagar her Egyptian maid, after Abram had dwelt ten years in the land of Canaan, and gave her to her husband Abram to be his [secondary] wife. And he had intercourse with Hagar, and she became pregnant; and when she saw that she was with child, she looked with contempt upon her mistress and despised her."

Women of the East were ashamed of their barrenness; they considered it to be a punishment from God. In order to escape the shame, the determined wives gave their handmaidens to their husbands as surrogate mothers and then raised the children as their own.

Hagar eventually gave birth to Ishmael, who was a constant reminder to Sarai of her impetuousness. Not only was Sarai barren, but she now had to contend with her husband's contemptuous secondary wife. Hagar displayed a superior attitude towards Sarai, jeering at her condescendingly and provoking her to jealousy.

Later, Sarai threw both Hagar and her son, Ishmael, out of her home. Not only had Hagar become a single mother, but her son Ishmael was without his father. And a broken hearted Abram was devastated over Sarai's decision, because he loved his son deeply.

When Abram was ninety-nine years old, God personally made a solemn pledge to him that he would multiply (have children) exceedingly. God changed his name from Abram (high, exalted father), to Abraham (father of a multitude). Sarai's name was changed to Sarah, which meant princess. God made them the father and mother of many nations.

God told Abraham that his wife, Sarah, would conceive her own son. Abraham was overjoyed at the prospect of he and Sarah having a son. However, he still made a final plea for his first born son, Ishmael. In Genesis 17:18, "And [he] said to God, Oh, that Ishmael might live before You!"

As God had promised, when Abraham was one hundred years old and Sarah was the ripe old age of ninety-nine, she conceived their son, Isaac. They were both elated, but a grief-stricken Abraham still often thought of Ishmael. Unfortunately, prior to their son Isaac's birth, Sarah had already taken matters into her own hands. She gave her handmaiden to her consenting husband and the results were disastrous.

Had Sarah prayed to God and waited for His response, she may have saved herself from much pain and disillusionment. Abraham, her husband, Hagar, her handmaid, and her stepson, Ishmael, would have been spared their harrowing pain, as well.

Hannah, on the other hand, was a woman who took the matters of her heart to God in prayer (I Samuels 1-2). She also loved and respected her husband, Elkanah. Hannah was a model woman, wife, and stepmother, and her life should be an inspiration to all women.

Quite the opposite, was Peninnah, Elkanah's other wife and the mother of Hannah's stepchildren. Although Peninnah bore Elkanah many children, he still loved Hannah so much more.

Peninnah was unhappy and apparently embittered because Elkanah did not love her. She seized every opportunity to vex and humiliate Hannah because of her barrenness. Her cruel insults had Hannah so grief-stricken that she lost her desire to eat. Nevertheless, Hannah refused to strike back at her.

Hannah's behavior troubled Elkanah a great deal. He entreated Hannah to stop grieving at once and to eat.

Instead of sulking and complaining about Peninnah, Hannah got up and ate, as her husband requested. Elkanah also went on to assure Hannah that she had no reason to grieve, because he loved her more than ten sons. (What man in his right mind would not love a submissive woman like Hannah?)

With prayer and supplication, she got down on her knees and made her request known to God.

There will always be women like Peninnah. Instead of being overcome by them, like Hannah, we must stay before the Lord in prayer.

Children are supposed to be a blessing conceived of two people in love. This was not the case with Elkanah and Peninnah. Nor is it the case with many couples today, who believe their marriages were a mistake. And while they may have been, the children that were conceived during those marriages were not mistakes. God ordained the birth of every child. People make mistakes, but people are not mistakes.

***

God honors marriages and He expects us to be faithful to our vows. But He does not expect us to subject ourselves to continuous and deliberate abuse.

After many parents have exhausted all possibilities of reconciliation, they get divorced. Some remarry. A stepparent is now brought into the lives of the children. And since this chapter is about stepmoms, I'll only refer to them.

In this triangular situation, the mothers, fathers, and stepmoms have a tremendous responsibility to the minor children. They are to shower them with as much love and minimal pain as possible.

There is nothing new under the sun, what is happening now has transpired in times past. Ex-wives towards stepmothers are displaying the same exalted attitude displayed by Peninnah towards Hannah (because of her childlessness). Unfortunately, it's done at the expense of the children.

***

The role of a stepmother is self-sacrificial; she has agreed to partake in rearing another woman's child. This is not always an easy task, considering many stepchildren exemplify the negative behavior of their mothers.

A Biblical example of this was the life of Ishmael. As he observed his mother's vulgar attitude towards his stepmother, he mimicked her (I Genesis 21). Like Ishmael, children often respond to their stepmoms according to the example set by their mothers. The divorce is difficult enough without the children feeling torn; they should not be forced to make choices between their mother, father and/or stepmother.

What is more, many divorced couples are unforgiving towards one another. Often the parents' hatred takes precedence over the children's happiness and well being. It is imperative for the children to understand that their parents were divorced from each other and not from them. Parents should put all negative feelings aside for the sake of their children.

Mothers often exhibit a negative behavior towards their children's stepmother. Both Peninnah and Hagar were antagonistic towards their children's stepmother. And more often than not, children mimic their parents.

On average, stepmothers are often completely ignored by their extended families. Such was the case with Hagar and Ishmael, neither of whom had any regards for Sarai, whatsoever.

***

The bulk of pressures and great demands of the stepmother are usually self-inflicted. For that reason, we must avoid extremes. Stepmothers must not be so dogmatic about pleasing their extended families that they find no pleasure in the relationships for themselves.

When the stepchildren refuse to accept you do not take it personally or internalize it. And remember it is their problem, not yours.

Another extreme is to withdraw altogether for fear of rejection and maltreatment. Even though the rejection of stepchildren may be uncomfortable, often their unapproachable behavior is merely a veneer. Do not fear their rejection but respect their boundaries.

***

Acceptance and **_Balance_** are key words that can keep stepmothers from oscillating emotionally. First, you must **_accept_** the fact that you are dealing with separate functioning, free will individuals (i.e., stepchildren). God has place within every one of us the ability - as well as the responsibility - to make our own choices. Therefore, if your stepchildren exercise their free will in choosing not to acknowledge you as their stepmother, simply accept that decision. Perhaps at a later time they may have a change of heart.

In the meantime, I suggest that you go on happily with your life and enjoy your husband.

Next, **_balance_** is the safeguard that will help you to abstain from being an over pleaser. Many wives are willing to go above and beyond their call to assure their husband's happiness. This may make them vulnerable in attempting to shoulder the burden of trying to appease everyone.

Furthermore, I strongly admonish stepmothers to stay off God's throne and on their knees. Prayer will keep you with an open heart, and burden-free.

The Serenity prayer can be your saving grace as it says it all: "God grant me the _Serenity_ to accept the things that I can not change, the _Courage_ to change the things that I can and the _Wisdom_ to know the difference."

Make this your creed and live by it. Remember Hannah, and do not internalize ill treatment or retaliate when gestures are made to deliberately antagonize you. Refrain from subjecting yourself to emotional instability. Also, support your husband's efforts to restore and maintain a healthy relationship with his children. Communicate openly and honestly with your husband, and do not bury disgruntled feelings.

When you suppress hurtful feelings, you often carry resentment.

Exhaust your efforts - but not yourself - in building a relationship with your stepchildren. After you have earnestly tried your best and yet they adamantly reject you, remember do not withdraw, but retreat. With an open heart and mind, you will be able to receive them if they wish to have a relationship with you.

The Bible states that we must live in peace with all men, if possible. If possible, attempt to have a rapport with the natural mother for the sake of your husband and stepchildren. If it is not possible, remember the word **acceptance**; accept her wishes, but do not take on her attitude as a threat.

Fear, real or imaginary, is generally empowered by both our perception and our response. Actually, most of the things we fear either never materialize or are beyond our ability to fix. Marie Curie said, *"Nothing in life is to be feared. It is only to be understood."*

When I was overwrought with an ongoing agitating situation, God gave me a simple, but profound solution. (This helped me to refocus and perhaps it may help you, as well.) God impressed upon my heart to get two blank sheets of paper and a pen. On the first sheet of paper, I drew stick people to represent my oppressors and a dollar bill (to represent money) from the top to the bottom of the sheet. Then on that same sheet, I drew a tiny stick person to represent God. This made me realize that I had blown my problems way out of proportion and made them much bigger than God.

On the second piece of paper at the bottom, I drew a dollar bill, and my oppressors as small stick people. Then I drew God from top to bottom, which put the entire situation back into its proper prospective.

Once again I saw that God is bigger than all my problems and all my fears. Meditating on the word of God was also helpful. I learned what I was experiencing—others had already survived. What's more, talking to other stepmothers can be a great source of support. Although the road of a stepmother may be paved with great challenge, your journey will be a whole lot easier with God's help. Prayer works! And remember, your wits end is a wonderful beginning for God.

S - Stepmothers are portrayed as crude
T - Their image is tarnished and shamed
E - Even the stepchildren won't accept them
P - Perhaps fairy tales are to blame
M - Maybe if all persons involved
O - Open their hearts they'll see
M - More than dad's new wife, a friend she'd love to be.

Dark Valley Days

One day at work while transacting business via telephone, I experienced difficulty hearing the lady with whom I was speaking. Her voice was barely audible.

Perplexed, I asked, "Can you hear me okay?"

"Yes I can hear you perfectly", she assured me.

As a lefty, I mindlessly pick up the telephone receiver and listen with my left ear. However, on that particular day, *unaware*, I placed the receiver to my right ear. Becoming more anxious and frustrated by the minute, I painstakingly tried to determine what the lady was saying.

It's pointless to continue this conversation, I exasperatingly thought. But just when I was about to hang up, I switched the telephone to my left ear and was able to hear her clearly.

Bewildered, I sat a long time at my desk mulling over what had transpired. I remembered a similar incident during a conversation with my dad a couple of year's prior. I initially thought I couldn't hear him clearly because we were talking long distance.

I asked, "Dad, are you hearing me okay?"

"Yea, baby, I can hear you just fine."

Obviously, I needed to see a doctor. Uninsured at the time, I went to the emergency room at a local hospital instead.

The physician on staff prescribed eardrops. Because I was not experiencing any pain, the problem was thought to have been resolved, though it had gone undetected for a couple of years.

When I had insurance, I decided to visit my primary physician. After he gave me the standard office hearing test, he sent me to HEARx, now known as the HEARUSA center for further testing.

Meanwhile, at HEARx (HEARUSA), I was given a hearing screening, basic comprehensive and pure tone audiometry, as well as other testing. I was strongly admonished by their staff person (who was extremely professional), to follow through with my upcoming doctor's visits. The man who tested me doubtless suspected that my own prognosis was considerably less severe than my problem. And because I was not experiencing any pain, he was probably correct.

Subsequent to HEARx, I met with an Ear, Nose, & Throat doctor, who sent me to a Magnetic Resonance Imaging (MRI) center for a head scan.

Late one evening, my ENT called me at home to inform me of his findings. The MRI confirmed that I had an Acoustic Neuroma, which was a conglomerate dimension of enhancing mass that was causing a mild compression on my right pontomedullary junction. In lay terms, a small mass of tissue (about the size of a dime) was compressing against my facial and balancing nerve. It was lodge on the right side at the base of my brain, which explained why I had difficulty hearing out of my right ear. The ENT said in and of itself the benign tumor was not a bad thing. It was, however, growing in an injurious area.

The doctor spoke calmly to avoid scaring the wits out of me. But having a tumor in my head and not knowing when it might possibly grow was extremely frightening. And while

I'll never forget the doctor's kindness, I utterly freaked out after speaking with him.

***

In spite of the recent diagnosis, my initial thoughts were not of dying and leaving my children. Nor did I immediately think of Willie, my recent husband and love of my life. What flashed across my mind like a bolt of lightning was the fear of not fulfilling my God given purpose. Something that I had not thought much about until faced with a life-threatening situation. And yet it was God who had placed that yearning for purpose in my heart.

In time I realized that the "dark valley days", initially thought to be a daunting experience, was actually a part of God's restorative plan for my life.

***

During our consultation, the Neurologist spoke quite candidly about the surgery he had recommended. He spoke of blood curdling side effects, which may have included (but were not limited to) strangling to death on my saliva, loss of serviceable hearing, and my right eye remaining permanently opened. And if that were not grueling enough, he also said that I could possibly lose my balance.

"How would that affect me, if I lost my balance?" I asked.

He responded, "You would walk like a drunken person."

Needless to say, I did not consider conventional surgery an option. But without surgery, the tumor would gradually grow and possibly cause the same devastation.

I seemed to be face with a no-win situation.

The Neurologist's description of the possible side effects sounded to me like a depiction from the movie, "The Bride of Frankenstein." And while making a mad dash from his office, I stumbled into a woman who resembled Frankenstein's wife. Apparently, the woman was one of the neurologist's patients who had had the surgery and suffered the side effects.

Dear God, please don't let anything awful like that happen to me, I prayed as I hurried from his office.

Scared stiff, I ran out to my car and shrieked uncontrollably, not just for myself but for the lady as well.

***

All the same, I continued my check ups. My husband was always at my side. We did exhaustive research: reading books, attending seminars, and learning of holistic and alternative curatives.

At one seminar we were taught how to obtain optimum health by fasting and juicing, which we did. As a result, we both lost a lot of weight and overall felt phenomenal. But these practices had no affect on the tumor in my head. Even so, I was greatly encouraged by the testimonies of others who rejected the death sentences of their doctors. Instead of giving up and throwing in the towel, they chose to take responsibility for their health and fight. And many of them won!

***

As I journeyed through the dark, maze-like depths of the valley, I learned the faithfulness and trustworthiness of Sovereign God. Although the 23rd Psalm was familiar scripture, He used it in countless ways to comfort me. At work on my radio, or at home in front of the television set, I heard it taught repeatedly.

Willie and I drove to Tallahassee, Florida, to visit a family member who was ill. When we stopped at a service station to fuel up, Psalm 23 was on the billboard. Without a doubt, God's goodness and mercy was literally following me.

After simultaneously bursting into tears and laughter, I bellowed, "Okay God I get your message."

Several long months had passed since the beginning of our ordeal, and we decided that a vacation would be nice. Willie and I went to Orlando, Florida, which was only a four-hour drive from home. Upon our arrival in the breathtakingly beautiful city, we checked in a hotel to *"play"* and even got a little rest. The following morning was so exquisite we decided to walk to the nearby restaurant, where we enjoyed hot coffee and pancakes topped with strawberries and whipped cream. Then off we went to Universal Studios where we had a blast. Our vacation was so pleasurable that we talked about it for days after.

About two weeks after our fun-in-the-sun vacation, gloom came over me again. Nearly a year had passed, and my healing seemed distant. I believed in the Sovereignty of God, but my faith failed me more often than I care to admit. Coming to terms with the fact that my healing depended upon God and not my having great faith was quite liberating, and comforting.

While commuting to work one morning, I fearfully asked my husband, "Honey, do you really believe God is going to heal me?"

He detected my uneasiness and calmly responded, "Yes, I believe God is going to heal you, but I think that it will happen when you least expect it."

Gradually my spirits lifted, I then asked, "Baby, would you consider moving to Orlando?"

And to my surprise, he was open to the idea, but suggested that we pray before making a decision.

***

The thought of relocating to Central Florida was innovative because neither one of us had ever lived outside of South Florida. We prayed, discussed the move at length, and doors began to swing wide open.

Our request for job transfers were both immediately approved, and through a local fellowship we were introduced to a couple who actually lived in Orlando. They generously offered us their guest bedroom whenever we were in the city apartment hunting.

In roughly two months we had found our dream apartment and were completely moved in. Willie went right to work, but for long exhausting hours.

Since I would not begin my job for nearly twelve weeks, I had lots of time on my hands. And being away from my family for the first time, I suffered mild depression and cultural shock. Preoccupation with my illness had mentally and physically worn me thin. Therefore, I was much in need of rest, relaxation, and restoration.

Eventually, I regrouped and immersed myself in dance aerobics, drinking juiced fruits and vegetables, and getting lots of sleep. While gradually adapting to the change, I learned to sit and be an audience of God, as He manifested Himself to me in wondrous ways. This was awesome, because I learned things in the valley that I would not have otherwise known had I not gone through it.

Ultimately, the illness I considered to be the worse thing that could have possibly happened gave me a new perspective on life. Patience replaced anxiety and fear was slowly but surely transforming into faith. Overall people seemed livelier and life much more interesting. Even the flowers seemed more colorful, the skies appeared bluer, and the stars shone brighter.

It was then that I made a conscience effort to stop taking life or people for granted. I found it hugely intoxicating, to drink from the fountain of life. And I overcame fear in the valley, as well. What is more, it became more apparent to me that God had my best interest at heart and was working on my behalf. Romans 8:28 - states, "We are assured and know that [God being a partner in their labor] all things work together and are [fitting into a plan] for good to and for those who love God and are called according to [His] design and purpose".

Generally, doctor visits made me feel anxious, but I had begun to feel a lot more relaxed. Living in Orlando, Florida, I needed to get new doctors and resume my routine check ups.

My primary physician had my medical records transferred from Fort Lauderdale, Fl. After learning the nature of my medical history, he sent me to a highly recommended ENT. And since I was adamantly opposed to conventional surgery, I went expecting little more than to learn if the tumor had grown. Instead, the ENT said, "Mrs. Johnson you are very lucky to be in Orlando, because we have the procedure to correct your problem."

As he spoke those long awaited words, I wanted to jump up and do somersaults around his office.

From the ENT, I was sent to a renowned neurosurgeon who recommended an outpatient surgery called Gamma Knife. This non-invasive laser surgery has minimal to no side effects. And unlike conventional surgery, because it is non-invasive, the nerves would not be severed.

Alas! the answer to our prayer had finally come *when we least expected it* and we were elated.

Even so, my valley experience had taught me when given a prescription or diagnosis, make an informed and intelligible decision. So we did do further research, but in our heart of hearts we believed that this was the answer from God. While searching the Internet for information on the gamma knife surgery, I learned that I had one of the top Neurosurgeons in the country.

Wow! Imagine that! It's just like God to give His children the absolute best.

***

The day finally arrived for my gamma knife surgery. As I approached the doorway of the Florida Hospital, I secretly wished that I were leaving instead of arriving. Quickly recanting that thought, I embraced the serenity of knowing that everything was under God's divine control.

As the doctors were monitoring and prepping me, Willie walked along side them as though he were a doctor. He asked so many questions; I was concerned that they would soon become annoyed with him. But actually they appeared to be quite patient and a bit humored.

After roughly four hours, which included watching television, eating cookies, drinking coffee, and finally the laser surgery, we were on our way home. Along the way we made a quick stop to buy fresh fish and rent movies from the video store. Other than a slight feeling of fatigue for a few days, it was as though I had not had surgery.

One week later, my husband's employer asked him to do a special assignment at their Sarasota, Florida branch. This meant that he would have to stay over because it was about a three-hour drive from where we lived. Willie informed his employer that he was not comfortable leaving me alone, since I had just recently had surgery. So, his company put us up in a luxurious hotel with a yachting view.

At the company's expense, we ate dinner every night at the restaurant of our choice. Every morning I indulged in fresh fruit and juice in the hotel dinning room. Afterwards I returned to our room and watched the beautiful yachts cruising past our window. Truly, the most strenuous thing that I did all day was pressing the buttons on the remote control. For a grand finale, God gave us room service, with the bill paid in full.

The "Dark Valley Days" experience enhanced my life and endowed me with much wisdom. After many years of quoting the 23rd Psalm, God gave me a firsthand experience of what it really meant to know Him as my Shepherd, and the countless benefits of being one of His sheep. Through the generosity of His giving, He taught me to be less selfish. Prior to this life transformation, I was rather self-absorbed.

For most of my life I feared death. But in the valley I came to appreciate that it had no power over me. God gives His sheep all that they need for their journey through the valley, even the faith to trust Him as their Shepherd.

Diamond in the Rough
Psalm 23

The Lord is my Shepherd [to feed, guide, and shield me], I shall not lack.

He makes me lie down in [fresh, tender] green pastures; He leads me beside the still and restful waters.

He refreshes and restores my life (my self); He leads me in the paths of righteousness [uprightness and right standing with Him not for my earning it, but] for His name's sake.

Yes, though I walk through the [deep, sunless] valley of the shadow of death, I will fear or dread no evil, for You are with me; Your rod [to protect] and Your staff [to guide], they comfort me.

You prepare a table before me in the presence of my enemies. You anoint my head with oil; my [brimming] cup runs over.

Surely or only goodness, mercy, and unfailing love shall follow me all the days of my life, and through the length of my days the house of the Lord [and His presence] shall be my dwelling place.

Java and a Friend

Genuine friendship is the thread that holds women together and keeps us from becoming emotionally unstitched. Since we are emotional creatures, we deeply yearn for female companionship. Women need friends with whom they can relate both emotionally and experientially.

Many men counselors are exceptionally skilled in their fields. However, their gender limits them to being sympathetic and not empathetic with women who are in an emotional crisis. Wise counsel is both needed and helpful, but nothing can replace the priceless benefit of friendship shared between two women. Tears, anger, guilt, and finally laughter over pippin' hot coffee with a friend works wonders to ease a woman's emotional pain.

During the darkest hours of a woman's deepest despair, she needs a shoulder to lean on and someone to care. Among her many possessions, be it diamonds or pearls, there's nothing more invaluable than coffee with the girls.

Feeling alone and forsaken as if you don't matter? That can easily be overcome with laughter and chatter. But to triumph over guilt after making a huge mistake, I recommend one friend and two slices of cheesecake.

A woeful heart can be eased and made calm, by calling your prayer partner and sharing the 23rd Psalm. Sadly, due to walls of impasse, such as jealousy and strife, many women forfeit this enrichment in life. Be it face to face, or via telephone, no truly fulfilled woman journeys through life entirely alone.

And when we go through menopause or have our menstruation, we generally feel the need for some serious ventilation.

The art of cultivating friendship overtime is something learned, while it can not be bought, with great effort it can be earned.

When I am feeling dispirited, a good friend is my choice, and nothing delights me like hearing her voice. Austin O'Malley wisely stated, "A homemade friend wears longer than one you buy in the market."

Doubtless, God gave women gabbing as a gift, because when we're down in the dumps, it generally gives us a lift. In my most disquieting moments of woeful despair, I call upon my friend and know she'll be there. We share our utmost secrets, in her I can confide, there is no room for masquerades, we give no place to pride. After prattling about pain, grief, and fears, we find the pathway to laughter, and joy replaces tears.

In the Bible, God uses the body as a metaphor to express the need of unity. I Corinthians 12:21 through 26 states, "And the eye is not able to say to the hand, I have no need of you, nor again the head to the feet, I have no need of you.

But instead, there is [absolute] necessity for the parts of the body that are considered the more weak. And those [parts] of the body which we consider rather ignoble are [the very parts] which we invest with additional honor, and our unseemly parts and those unsuitable for exposure are treated with seemliness (modesty and decorum).

Which our more presentable parts do not require. But God has so adjusted (mingled, harmonized, and subtly proportioned the parts of) the whole body, giving the greater honor and richer endowment to the inferior parts which lack [apparent importance], so that there should be no division or discord or lack of adaptation [of the parts of the body to each other], but the members all alike should have a mutual interest in and care for one another."

And to further express our need of unity, I will refer to women as diverse parts of the body. A woman, who's a hand, will indubitably help if she can. While another who's an ear, when desired will draw near. Also, the leg that's leaped high hurdles in life can encourage the newcomer, who's a recent wife. But the mouth of wise counsel is needed for sure, when life is more than one can endure. We all need each other and must play a part, in helping to heal one another's injured heart. The leg can not bend without the knee, and without the eye the face can not see. All gifts were given with love and care, not to selfishly hoard, but to amorously share.

Women with tearful eyes, who have fallen apart, often sought God's help to heal their hearts. And when help arrives in ways unexpected, it's common for them to easily reject it. But in God's Sovereign plan to integrate us as one, He uses common people to get His work done.

Psalm 46:1, clearly states, "God is our Refuge and Strength [mighty and impenetrable to temptation], a very present and well-proved help in trouble."

God's numerous ways to answer a cry, are greater in number than stars in the sky. And when we entreat Him on bended knee, His ears are opened to our heart's plea. But whom He uses is of His own volition, and He does not have to ask us for our permission.

The pursuit of a perfect friendship may prove to be endless, and you may find yourself alone and friendless. If a friend's motives are pure towards God and you, even though she's not perfect, she will certainly do.

I believed a perfect friend to be quite a catch, but once I entered the relationship, it became a mixed match. And if you both love God with all your hearts, He knows how to fix your broken parts. Authentic friendship is as delicate as a gentle rose, so sweet the fragrance that sweeps beneath your nose.

Same as a garden, cultivating a friendship requires lots of maintenance work. For both, you need the appropriate tools as well as a good foundation to sow upon. Gardeners need rich soil, gardening tools, water, and appropriate seeds for the harvest they wish to grow. Cultivating a friendship requires tools of respect, honesty, and selflessness. For the foundation, compatibility, which means finding a friend with whom you share common interest.

For instance, I am a married woman with adult children, grandchildren, and stepchildren. Also, I am currently going through menopause, which can prove to be extremely perplexing at times. And because I am a Christian, I most certainly want the feed back of a friend from a Biblical perspective.

Although you may not share all things in common, it's imperative that you share most.

Thoughtfulness and kindness are to friendship what rain and sunshine are to a garden. Even so, a friend like anyone else will disappoint you at times. At those times, simply remember to water your friendship with forgiveness.

The bond of friendship should be treated in some ways like the union of marriage—with commitment and trustworthiness. Things spoken privately should be kept confidential. It is equally important to respect each other's individuality and right to differ in opinion, which brings a smorgasbord of emotional support to the friendship.

Generally, women need to work through oodles of emotions to get their issues resolved. Even though some of us are married, we still need the emotional support of others.

At times, I inadvertently displaced my husband for a soul-mate friend. In retrospect, I should have realized how tedious that was for him when I noticed him hyperventilating. During football season, he wanted nothing more than to be a couch potato and enjoy the games. But I rambled on with repetitious dialogue like a talking Chatty Kathy doll.

To his credit, he tried to act interested. But like a fish out of water, he was definitely displaced! I eventually *wised-up* and let my fish off the hook.

Many husbands lavish their wives with love and support, but they are not substitutes for female companionship. Men's and women's needs differ. While most wives are marathon talkers, their husbands barely make it off the starting line. Some husbands make an earnest effort to communicate with their wives; nevertheless, chitchat is not their forte.

In certain instances, wives certainly need to communicate with their husbands. However, girl talk should be exclusively reserved for girl friends.

***

In times gone by, I felt alone and friendless. I have since come to realize that to have a friend, I had to first learn to be a friend. Fear of possible betrayal caused me to give up rather quickly on potential friends.

Walls of jealousy, contention, envy and strife, along with ethnicity and cultural differences have been long time barriers between women. But have you noticed the most beautiful flowerbeds are the ones that are arrayed with multi-colors?

The outer appearance is merely the packaging, not the contents of that individual. We must learn to embrace our differences, which all come from God.

Blessed are women who are experiencing soul mate friendships, for their lives will be more enriched as a result. Bring down those walls that prevent you from enjoying the gift of friendship God desires you to have. A friend can be a ray of light during your dark journey through the tunnels of life.

Java, Sister?

Enthralled by the tailored suit, my flawless makeup and analogous jewelry
I see you, as you glance from a distance

In appearance your assumption is that I am a woman who's self possessed
Perhaps you've formed an opinion in your mind

Maybe you think you know me, near me you don't want to be
You rush pass in haste, wary not to make eye contact

I was kinda hoping that perhaps you would spare me a moment of your time

Java, Sister? Even lunch if you desire, I jus' needed someone to chat with

What you see is not me, what you can't see
is who I be
My body's wrapped in extravagant attire
But I am the soul with well kept secrets peeping out at you through the windows of my eyes

And when a river of tears descends and locks beneath my chin
My soul is speaking a universal language
I AM HURTING...

Overweight?

For many women, a sculpted body and a youthful appearance are to die for. Small fortunes have been invested in liposuction and breast reconstruction. Masses of women visit cosmetic counters to purchase eye creams for crows' feet, while others are breaking a sweat at the gym to shed those unwanted pounds.

Obsession with weight loss has driven many women to developing Anorexic Nervosa or Bulimic Nervosa. Perfectionism and low self-esteem are common traits among more than 80% of young women who are anorexic.

Countless young women are emaciated from eating disorders and starvation. Sadly, without treatment, a startling 20% or more of those people struggling with eating disorders will die.

Despite the aimless efforts of diets, enhancers, and reconstructions, perfectionism resulting from damaged emotions is the primary cause of many women being overweight.

***

In my younger (and thinner) days, despite the opinion of others, I felt that I was skinny and unattractive. The scales in the various grocery stores dictated the fate of my superficial happiness. Instead of appreciating my petite figure, I desperately wanted to gain weight. Emotionally, I was either soaring to the mountaintop or plummeting to the ocean floor, based upon that day's reading on the scale.

Working dogmatically at camouflaging my insecurities: I applied my make-up flawlessly, made sure my accessories complimented my attire, and styled my hair for hours at a time. (Actually, with time and practice, I became a perfectionist at perfectionism.) My appearance revealed an impeccable woman, self-possessed and well satisfied. But although I appeared to have had it all together, a nagging sense of worthlessness incessantly bombarded me.

Appearance does not always reveal the true self; however, it may reflect self-image. Weight loss, cosmetics, and enhancers are fabulous, but they will not cure low self-worth or perfectionism. An attempt to resolve this emotional problem with one's outer appearance is comparable to extinguishing a forest fire with a bucket of water.

Perfectionism is an act of excessively striving to satisfy an unquenchable thirst and/or to meet inaccessible demands. The out-of-control individual who exemplifies this type of obsessive behavior is known as a perfectionist.

Lack of affirmation, nurturing, and emotional abuse suffered during childhood often diminishes self-worth and promotes perfectionism. Typically, due to lack of identity, perfectionists strongly feel the need to be characterized by their appearances, accolades, and accomplishments.

The subtle character traits of the perfectionist are more difficult to detect. For instance, the outward show of an exceptionally hard-working employee may be a workaholic in disguise. The unrelenting pursuit of identity through work efforts often results in workaholics overexerting themselves. The addict is then placed in a notably vulnerable position, given that the predatory employer (who lacks thoughtfulness) takes advantage of the situation by allowing the workaholic to burn the candle on both ends.

The emotional boundaryless perfectionist/addict experiences difficulty differentiating who they are from what they do. Many place their families on the back burner as they climb the corporate ladder of success (for identity purposes). Perfectionism destroys families and often physically, mentally, and emotionally debilitates its victim, and in some cases, claims their lives.

What is more, the sadistic upbringing of many celebrities has actually contributed to their fame and fortune. Their pursuit of significance and identity has driven some to become well known entertainers. However, despite their material comfort, beneath the surface they are merely broken people in need of emotional healing. In fact, countless performers are disclosing the appalling abuses that they suffered during their childhood.

Devoted fans has placed various performers on pedestals and made idols (gods) of them. In spite of this, when their emotional injuries cause these idols to behave abnormally, they are harshly judged by some of the same fans, who had previously worshipped them.

Among the common traits of perfectionism are low self-esteem and self-depreciation. Although the perfectionist tenaciously strives to attain self worth through external efforts, their pain is emotional and internal. And since the core of the problem is out of sight, it often goes undetected ... or more importantly, unresolved. As a result of their excruciating pain, perfectionists will more than likely pursue someone or something to bring them momentary comfort.

True to the addictive nature, the perfectionist lacks self-restraint. Their excessive behavior causes an addiction to — rather than the gratification from — the person or substance. Foods, alcohol, tobacco, sex, and drugs (to name a few) are all entities that have been abnormally used by the perfectionist. Initially these things may provide some gratification, but often the individual becomes addicted and entrapped.

To offset the devastation of my personal pain, I became a co-dependent addict. I was addicted to the feeling that someone "loved" me. This so-called love was what I felt I needed and quickly became a form of self-medication to ease my pain. I always seemed to feel as if I could never get enough of that person. However, as with the benefit of hindsight, I realize that it was never love, but rather that very same co-dependency that I was experiencing.

Apprehended and doing life-long sentences, addicts are confined within their own emotional prison. Although emotional prison bars are not visible, they are confining, nonetheless.

Furthermore, the body and the soul are interdependent and must both be worked on simultaneously for optimal health. Self-love motivates us to keep our bodies and souls healthy. But the perfectionist lacks self-love, and regardless of their many accomplishments and accolades, they tend to have a derogatory perception of themselves. Working through the emotional pain of your past is the only way to overcome low self-esteem, which leads to perfectionism, and then becomes an addictive behavioral pattern.

I have been blessed to find my identity in Christ, which means my perception of who I am, is based upon the Word of God.

Millions of Americans suffer from various eating disorders, and some are not even aware that they have a food addiction. Unlike illegal drugs, alcoholism, or sexual addictions that are more readily diagnosed, eating disorders may initially go unnoticed. Nevertheless, it is as devastating and deadly as any other addiction. An eating disorder is not to be taken lightly because it involves food (which may seem harmless) and not excessive amounts of alcohol or illegal drugs. Bear in mind that the addiction is not the substance used to medicate and bring momentary comfort, but rather the psychological displacement of the addict.

It took me *more* than half my life to realize there was a great deal more to me than how I looked. And who I am on the inside is what really counts. The obsession I had with my outward appearance was a clear-cut indication of something not functioning properly inwardly.

Caring about our appearance is one thing, but to be driven and out of control means there is an obvious or subtle emotional issue within that needs to be resolved.

The chapter "Overweight", in and of itself, is not curative of any disorder. However, the sole purpose of it is to evoke awareness so you can get the proper help that's needed. Contingent upon the severity of your emotional injury, you may require professional help. Also, pray and seek God's guidance on any and all restorative plans you are pursuing.

Remember! Do not allow your past to **_shape_** your future. Know that there is so much more to you than meets the eye.

Laurette Taylor Johnson
Women

Women are the salt of the earth,
uniquely divine
Our strength unmatchable,
we are one of a kind

As forceful as a rainstorm,
yet gentle as the breeze,
Limbs bow in our honor,
as we stroll beneath the trees.

Lovers by heart, like us
there's indisputably no other
Strikingly beautiful,
no matter our shape, size, or color.

God's gifts unopened
(Abortion)

God created man, but the Bible states that He took special care in the making of the woman. This is the reason our bodies are voluptuously formed and shapely. Genesis 2:22 states, "And the Lord God fashioned into a woman the rib, which He had taken from a man, and brought her to the man."

A woman's body has multiple functioning and distinguished parts designed to both give and receive. In the heat of passion during their times of intimacy, a woman's body receives from her husband. And after conception, she (in most cases) gives to her child.

The Word of God also admonishes us, as parents, to bring our children up in the love and admonition of the Lord. Generally babies are cherished when they are born into an atmosphere of such love and acceptance. Some mothers, with elation and gratitude, welcome their unborn as a gift. But there are others who perceive their unborn as unwelcome intruders. This is terribly unfortunate for the unborn who may be entering life-threatening territory.

Girls who were not loved and affirmed during their formative years often grow up to be inadequate and bewildered women. Many of them find the prospect of parenting to be staggering.

I must admit when I saw my newborn for the first time, I was frightened beyond words. *What in the world am I going to do with this baby?* I pondered. Although he was beautiful, I was seventeen - both young and incompetent.

Pregnancy among teens was sporadic during my school days... or so I thought. I later learned that abortions had actually been around for quite some time. And just because many of my peers were not having babies did not necessarily mean they were not getting pregnant. Even so, as a frightened teenager, by the grace of God I still decided to give birth to my baby. (Carl Sandburg said, "A baby is God's opinion that the world should go on.")

Since there is an emotional attachment between the mother and her unborn, I am inclined to believe that the baby may sense when (s)he is unwanted.

***

In the first chapter of the book of Luke, the angel Gabriel told the Virgin Mary that she would conceive a child (Jesus). And he went on to say, "And listen! Your relative Elizabeth in her old age has also conceived a son, and this is now the sixth month with her who was called barren."

Elizabeth was pregnant with child who was later known as John(the baptizer). He became the forerunner for Mary's son, Jesus.

After hearing the good news about Elizabeth and certainly wanting to share her own, Mary hastened to the hill-country town of Judah.

Upon her arrival at Zacariah's home, Mary graciously greeted his wife and her cousin, Elizabeth.

As soon as she heard Mary's voice, Elizabeth felt the baby leap in her womb. (This is evidence the unborn is emotionally connected and instinctively aware of his mother's emotions. When the unborn is thought to be an unwelcome intruder, (s)he will more than likely, sense their mother's rejection.)

***

Some abortions are treated as casually as a common cold. Society at large has virtually become desensitized to abortions. And often, parents express little or no remorse afterwards. What's more, after an abortion many women simply go about their normal routines as though nothing of any importance has taken place.

An unplanned pregnancy does not give good reason for an abortion. As many other women with unplanned pregnancies, my mother conceived me at an inopportune time.

As a single parent, my mother was barely keeping her head above water. She single-handedly raised me. As the youngest, I often told her that I wanted a baby sister or brother.

Momma would respond, "Hush, my dear, and be glad you're here. You almost missed the ship!"

Perhaps she may have very well considered abortion. But I thank God she did not abort me.

***

Out of my five children, I did not have a single planned pregnancy. I went to great lengths to prevent getting pregnant. But of the different methods of birth control I tried, they either caused me pain or side effects. I was allergic to the birth control pills. And perhaps due to my tilted uterus, the IUD (intrauterine device) caused me considerable pain. With soundness of mind, I can now say that abstinence would have been the sure-fire way to avoid pregnancy. Except at the time, I was in and out of abusive relationships and there was no stability in my life for a baby.

At times, I thought long and hard about having an abortion. But after careful consideration, I concluded that it was not my decision to determine if another human being should live or die. The unborn—like his mother—has a right to life. Planned pregnancy or not, abortion should never be an option.

This is not a judgment call. It is a wake up call!

The good news is that God forgives all sins, even the sin of taking someone else's life. And He will heal our broken hearts and contrite spirits. Everyone has sinned, and all sins weigh the same in God's eyes. But, God forgives.

Jesus was the wisest, purest, and most powerful man on earth. Yet, He was the humblest and most forgiving. Jesus demonstrated that when evil men who sought His opinion on stoning an adulterous woman confronted Him. The Law of Moses stated that any women caught in the act of adultery were to be put to death by way of stoning [John 8 & Deuteronomy 22:22-24].

Jesus wisely dispelled the crowd by saying he who is without sin cast the first stone at her. John 8:9 states that they listened to Him, and then they began going out, conscience-stricken, one by one, from the oldest down to the last one of them.

Finally Jesus was alone with the woman in the center of the court. John 8: 10-11 says: "When Jesus raised Himself up, He said to her, Woman, where are your accusers? Has no man condemned you?"

She answered, "No one, Lord"

And Jesus said, "I do not condemn you either. Go on your way and from now on sin no more."

Although Jesus deeply loves the sinner, he does not approve of the act of sin itself.

***

Some women have had multiple abortions and may wonder if they are worthy of forgiveness. The answer? An emphatic yes!

In Matthew 18:21- 22: "Then Peter came up to Him and said, Lord, how many times may my brother sin against me and I forgive him and let it go? [As many as] up to seven times?

Jesus answered, "I tell you, not up to seven times, but seventy times seven!"

Although God freely forgives, an abortion grieves His heart. Nevertheless, if you have had an abortion and your heart is overwhelmed with guilt and self-condemnation, remember God is bigger than your heart. And His grace and mercy is more than sufficient for you.

Ephesians 1:7 states, "In Him we have redemption (deliverance and salvation) through His blood, the remission (forgiveness) of our offenses (shortcomings and trespasses), in accordance with the riches and the generosity of His gracious favor."

God lavishes every one of His children with grace, mercy and forgiveness. If you are not His child, you can be ... for the mere asking. Simply invite Jesus into your heart and ask Him to forgive you for all sins you have committed.

1 John 1,9 states, "If we [freely] admit that we have sinned and confess our sins, He is faithful and just (true to His own nature and promises) and will forgive our sins [dismiss our lawlessness] and [continuously] cleanse us from all unrighteousness [everything not in conformity to His will in purpose, thought, and action]."

Because God loves me so graciously, I am motivated to also love Him.

***

Healing and restoration involves dealing with dormant pain and internalized guilt. When pain is too traumatic, we tend to suppress rather than deal with it. There is some truth in the saying, no pain no gain.

Preventing ourselves from grieving only prolongs the process of healing ... in some cases, indefinitely. Therefore, you must allow the pain to resurface; embrace it when it does.

Here are some steps that may help you unlock that dormant pain.

1. Name and imagine holding your baby in your arms as you sit in a quiet place.
2. Call your baby by his/her name. Explain why you had the abortion and your frame of mind when you did.
3. Ask for your baby's forgiveness.
4. Pray, ask, and receive God's forgiveness.
5. Forgive yourself.
6. Join a support group and get Christian counseling.
7. Read and meditate upon Scriptures involving comfort and forgiveness.

***

Great healing is found in the multitude of counsel. God's *Gift Unopened* is dedicated to hurting woman all over the world. My first-born died at the tender age of two (from what seemed an untimely death) and not an abortion. His name was James Arthur Hardwick III, and we called him

Poncho. His presence shall be greatly missed as long as I live.

Although I never had an abortion, I do not stand in judgment of women, who have, because I realize this could have just as easily been me.

As a final point, for women who may be contemplating abortions please consider two important facts: A distressing lifestyle may be *alterable*. An abortion is *unalterable*.

God gave me four other gifts: Kelton, Michael, Angela, and Curtis. I am eternally grateful for each of them.

***

I pray that you find comfort in knowing that all sins weigh the same, and all babies go back to heaven's domain. After the death of David's son he said, "I shall go to him, but he shall not return to me." (II Samuel 12:23.)

A Gift from God

*An unborn child is God's gift
in heavenly wrappings,
Serenaded with songs
and the sounds of angels clapping.
Cheering on this bundle of joy,
Which soon may come to be
One of God's greatest gifts
sent down to humanity.*

***

In Remembrance of My son, Poncho

Walking fast, running through puddles
Leaping high ... that's Poncho!
Fighting hard, being sweet,
a good night's kiss -
That's Poncho, too!
Bubbly smile, sparking eyes,
an Afro that's really neat,
Strawberry lips,
so very sweet.
Poncho left for heaven
On the wings of a dove
To join hands with the angels
Serving up above.

Men Oughta Pause
(Menopause)

Menopause is a life-changing experience for women. It is a time of challenge that can be both refreshing and renewing. I equate it to God's gift of a second chance to women, an opportunity to get our lives off the shelf and live them.

A woman's life is sacrificial as she devotes all of herself, time, and energy to rearing her children, and in some cases, her *husband*. Few women consider caring for their loved ones as self-sacrificing, because home is where their hearts are. Moreover, menopause shouts out to the woman, demanding that for the first time her undivided attention be turned toward herself.

Most women are excellent at caring for their homes and families. However, those same women are generally negligent in giving themselves quality time without feeling guilty. We as women will all experience menopause and we will only get to do it once. There are no time-outs for rehearsals; we simply have to go with the flow, learning as we go. And although it is wisdom to get educated regarding menopause, chances are your experience will be a personal one.

Menopause affects women in different ways and to different degrees. Some of the symptoms are hot flashes, mood swings, vaginal dryness, decreased libido, and insomnia. And while some women suffer minimum discomfort, others may suffer severely. Also, many women may be at a higher risk level for osteoporosis, heart disease, breast cancer, and cardiovascular disease, to name a few.

If you are at a higher risk, and depending on the severity of your symptoms, you may need to consult your gynecologist. Initially, my doctor recommended prescription hormones. But after researching, I was concerned about the possible side effects. During my doctor's visits, I found that my gynecologist was so busy that he would simply diagnose me and toss me a prescription. Much to my chagrin, I would leave his office as though I understood what he had said, when I honestly did not. *It would be a terrible imposition to ask too many questions*, I often thought to myself. But I thank God that I stopped that nonsense. Now even after he explains, I question him until I fully understand.

I write on menopause not as a medical expert, but rather from an emotional and experiential viewpoint. In order to make an informed decision regarding the most appropriate and safe regimen for me, I gathered information from professionals, via doctor visits, books, and the Internet (which has a world of medical information). From this material, I concluded that the best course of therapy for me was natural.

After a visit to my local nutritional center, I decided to take phyto-estrogen, which is a natural alternative. I also take vitamins, exercise, and drink herbal teas. And I juice a variety of fruits and vegetables. Menopause is often referred to as *the change,* and requires that we make some changes. While it is not necessary to be an expert on menopause, we are responsible for our emotional and physical well being.

Additionally, the *"men ought to pause"* for a moment with their wives to learn what is transpiring in their lives. Likewise, if the children are of age that they can comprehend, they also need to be informed. Chances are they will be, since women generally go through menopause as their children are approaching early adulthood. Because this often proves to be a perplexing time in a woman's life, she needs lots of love, support, and understanding.

More often than not, the hormonal imbalance will cause women to have mood swings and mixed emotions of sorts. As a result, we may display a behavior that contradicts our true character. Typically, when that happens, most women are crushed emotionally.

This is a life-altering time for a woman that must not be ignored or taken lightly. It may prove to be a difficult time for her loved ones, as well. However, it can be more easily handled with understanding, and acts of loving support from her husband and children.

As menopausal women, we should be the recipients of lots of pampering at this time in our lives ... from our family members and ourselves. After spending many years nurturing and rearing our children, as well as loving and catering to the needs of our husbands, we deserve to be served. This is the perfect time for a woman to become acquainted with herself and learn what a magnificent creature she truly is.

***

Over time, some women seem to almost become non-existent as we completely ignore our own wants and needs. However, many menopausal women have gone back to school and earned degrees for their long-desired careers. Some endeavor to become entrepreneurs — many with success. Moreover, menopause forces women to look at and within themselves, as their bodies express needs that refuse to be ignored any longer.

Quite frankly, the timing could not be more perfect. The adult children are usually grown and out of the house. This is such a wonderful time for a woman to embrace herself, and maximize her potential in life. Have a fabulous time with yourself and do daring things that you may have previously thought unimaginable. Make people look at you and say, "Well I never thought she would have done something like that!"

I admit, in the beginning I thought briefly of the opinions of others concerning the changes I dared to make. Fortunately for me, it was only a fleeting thought that was soon dismissed.

Becoming in touch with my inner self made me feel like a star on center stage. Some of us rediscover ourselves, while many others discover themselves for the first time. Occasionally, I felt as though I were in an uphill struggle; other times, I felt divinely superb. Now, I am learning to enjoy my life in ways that I never imagined possible. I do fun things, such as trying different shades of makeup and fashionable haircuts. I traded my reading glasses for a variety of color contacts. (At times I wore hazel or gray, other times, amethyst.)

During menopause, it was not enough to merely exist. I found that I needed to live, purposely. For a getaway, my husband and I often checked into a hotel near the ocean. As we sat on the hotel's balcony enjoying the ocean's view, we ate shrimp, clams, oysters, and other shellfish. I changed careers from working in an office for the state to becoming a beauty consultant. The cosmetic industry that employed me required me to take training classes, and I learned how to apply make-up flawlessly. They gave me tons of cosmetics; I played with them all.

The ocean's view, colored contacts, fashionable haircuts, and cosmetics are all things that brought me pleasure. Discover your own passion with a childlike heart, and enjoyably pursue it.

Along with my other undertakings, I wrote this book, which is something that has burned within my heart for many years. I have found a great deal of healing in venting my feelings through writing.

Even if your aspiration is not to become an author, you may still find it quite rewarding to keep a journal. The decision to write this book was born from my passion to help hurting women with guilty hearts ... so that they may have an easier journey, as they travel the roads that I have already traveled (thus far).

***

There may be times when you experience aching joints and pains that seem to just creep up on you all at once. This is the perfect opportunity to privilege your body with optimal health. (I walked the track from three to five miles every day, or used an aerobics tape, which is equivalent to a four-mile walk. As a result, I am the benefactor of good health and a great body. I feel fabulous.)

As menopause challenged me to get healthier, I found that I felt better than I had in my entire life, even when I was much younger. I view it as a gift from God, rewarding me with a new life for the years of nurturing that I gave to my family. And while I did enjoy caring for my family, I am equally enjoying caring for myself.

Initially, I was afraid to learn about menopause ... partly because of things that I had been told. One friend told me, "Just don't think about it," as though thinking about it would cause some psychological ramifications. But I was staying up all night with night sweats and insomnia. My emotions were jumping around as though they were on a trampoline. It was then that I decided it would be in my best interest to learn about the needs and demands of my body. In my case, ignorance was certainly not bliss.

What is more, I was an excessive coffee drinker — to the point that I was addicted to it. And if I tried to quit, my body would go through a withdrawal cycle. Caramel

Cappuccino Latte coffee was my favorite, and I bought the cubes of cappuccino caramel candies, to eat while I drank my coffee. Needless to say, I was having hot flashes by the minute. And I had not experienced the luxury of a good night's sleep for quite some time. Even sleeping pills would not put me to sleep; instead, I just felt even more tired and restless. My body rejected everything that was not good for it and had an undesirable reaction to certain foods and beverages.

For insomnia, walking helped tremendously and I also replaced my daily intake of caffeine with peppermint, chamomile, or spearmint teas with honey (which were all very delicious and stimulating). Initially, I had insomnia so acutely that I would also take valerian root to aid me in getting to sleep. At night, I often looked over at my husband who could sound off a good snore as soon as his head hits the pillow.

Now, late at night, even if I wanted to stay up and watch a movie, I could not; most of the time I fall asleep effortlessly.

A woman's metabolism slows down a great deal at this time and we have a tendency to panic for fear of that "ghastly middle-age spread." I found that eating healthy foods and exercising kept me balanced at a desirable weight. (I suggest if you are experiencing any of these symptoms, get busy and put together a plan that will work for you.) I started out using natural alternatives. Later, when I entered the more advanced stages of menopause, I occasionally took prescription hormones, but never on an on going basis. As I was concerned about the side effects.

***

Being well informed of the possible side effects of medication is something I learned while working with the elderly. Many of the clients had multiple health problems, which they said resulted from the side effects of their medications. Some even claimed that they had always eaten fruits, vegetables, fish, and poultry to maintain good health. They had neither smoked cigarettes nor drunk alcohol. Often the side effects, I am inclined to believe, can be more detrimental than the actual illness.

Make sure that you are comfortable with both your diagnosis and your plan of treatment. Ask questions and get second opinions, if necessary. In some cases, you may not have an option. However, when an option is available carefully select the one that's best suited for you. It's your life! Aren't you worth it?

***

At a time when I feared my life could possibly fall apart, I soon learned that I had only just begun to live. Having a romantic evening at home with my husband meant occasionally sipping wine in front of the fireplace. And while I was at the store purchasing a bottle of Chardonnay, the cashier asked me for I.D. She was very apologetic, as she looked at the date of birth on my driver's license. She quickly looked at me again and said "Wow! You look great!"

At that time, I was one month shy of my 48th birthday. I smiled and replied, "Oh no problem. God bless you."

***

To look good is awesome; to feel great is equally rewarding.

Fortunately, I have a supportive husband; it is really a plus not to have a lot of stress in your life. If you have stress, as we all do, learn to manage it. Although the adult children were out of my house physically, learning to let go of my daughter, Angela, and my grandchildren, Lakenyai and Laurence, emotionally was quite difficult. I worried about them constantly and was always in unrest. My unnerving emotions forced me to release them, just as my body demanded that I abstain from excessive portions of unhealthy foods.

During one visit with my daughter, Angela and my grandchildren, my menstrual cycle (which I had not seen in a while) came on. And my tap-dancing emotions made me extremely sensitive, to put it mildly. For the most part, Angie and I had had a pretty good relationship. However, one night during that visit, I told her that I felt unwelcome in her home. She immediately burst into tears, and I was swept away with guilt. After putting my feelings into words, I realized how preposterous it sounded.

Without delay, I got on the telephone with my sister, who is older than I am. She explained how emotional changes during menopause could cause you to say or do things out of the ordinary. But despite my awkward attempt to explain to Angela what was going on with me, our relationship was momentarily dampened.

That experience taught me an invaluable lesson of replacing self-condemnation with self-forgiveness, which kept me from being consumed by guilt during my low times.

Women are experts at nurturing others but amateurs when it comes to nurturing ourselves. For that reason, self-love is foreign to most of us.

***

Because menopause is a journey, it's imperative to map out a plan so that you will get through it with the least amount of interruptions. In the past I seldom drank water. Now, for the detoxification of my body and beautiful skin I drink it often. I find that it both refreshes and revitalizes me.

Life is blissful, and I am enjoying every moment of it. The streaks of highlights in my hair are evidence of that. I went out and bought myself a toe ring and an anklet, because I am pampering myself from head to toe. Also, I am sporting a thumb ring, given to me by my daughter. Okay, I am not totally out of control, but I am enjoying myself immensely.

Willie showers me with compliments and dances with me when I am in the kitchen cooking. The fact that I love myself and I am feeling good about me also makes him the benefactor of this royal treatment.

***

Life is an adventure and so is cooking gourmet dinners. I avoid cooking a lot of red meats, but occasionally we will have some nice juicy steaks. I grill salmon filets with honey and teriyaki sauce, or Cornish hens drenching with lemon juice and dried red pepper. I steam broccoli, cook cabbage sauteed with lots of onions and garlic, and all sorts of scrumptious dishes.

Single women can maximize their lives and have a blast during menopause as well. Surround yourself with positive, affirming people. Read lots of helpful material, and do fun things. Take long bubble baths, light up some candles and play your favorite music. Learn to be your own best friend, and be more understanding and less judgmental of yourself.

Equally important, the menopausal woman must accept that she is also changing physically. Do not set yourself up for disappointment by expecting to wear that size 3 dress that you wore before "*the change*." Also, talk with other women about their experiences with menopause.

At the onslaught of menopause, household chores frustrated me a great deal. My mind told me I could do them, but my body protested and defiantly disagreed. Back then, I was mentally and emotionally exhausted whenever I over-exerted myself physically.

My dad, who was visiting me, noticed that I was warring against myself. Daddy explained what he knew about menopause. He said, "Honey, your body is changing, and you are not the same as you use to be."

Of course, I knew that someday I would experience menopause ... somewhere down the road. Up until that point, I simply had not given it much thought. Now that I have a course of therapy (which I am committed to), I am more physically capable and also more emotionally sound. And I no longer feel the urgency to get my household chores done within a certain time frame.

Be courageous and daring. This is your time. Jump into life with a new attitude and land on your feet in style. Create a new and gorgeous you with a glamorous hairdo, makeup, and a new wardrobe. And don't sit around waiting for the affirmation of others; affirm yourself.

More importantly, let the word of God affirm you. He has some wonderful things to say about you personally, and it is all in His word (the Bible). He knows you better than anyone else (including you); after all, He is your Creator. God says that you are wonderfully and fearfully made and you are the apple of His eye.

Men Ought to Pause

*Men ought to pause, at your beauty divine,
Magnificent and unique, you're one of a kind.*

*They ought to pull out a chair, and offer you a seat
You're the most awesome creature a man will ever meet.*

*When you're feeling unhappy he should be right there,
Listening to every word intently, showing that he care.*

*Don't settle for a man, who will offer you less,
You are God's creation, and you deserve His best.*

Who am I?

The superlative woman of the millennium makes a breathtaking fashion statement with her wardrobe of hats. Each hat that she wears epitomizes her many roles. Throughout the course of her day, she sports them all. She has a wife's hat, a mother's hat, a maid's hat, and career woman's hat to name a few. She strives tirelessly to accomplish to perfection all of her tasks. But as a *jack of so many trades*, chances are she's not likely to master any of them. *The artist who aims at perfection in everything achieves it in nothing* (Delacroix).

Inadvertently, nurturing mothers rarely spend time on themselves; they presumably feel that their quality time is better served elsewhere. As a general rule, no one plans a curriculum on self-negligence or how to be a fanatical pleaser. However, social order does dictate to women that their sole purpose in life is to serve. After all, many of us are encircled with needy family members, friends, and co-workers. And since women are natural nurturers, most of us actually enjoy nurturing. But masses of us tend to go way overboard, especially as it pertains to our family members.

The dis-ease of over-pleasing is a universal dysfunction among many women. Typically, we are found on every corner of the earth busily doing for others (i.e., family members) what they are capable of doing for themselves. We engage ourselves in the catch-22 of excessively giving. And yet our futile attempt to meet the endless demands of others generally encourages them to expect this of us.

Consequently, as we give more, more is demanded of us.

The less time we invest in ourselves, the less we have to give to anyone else. By and large, a woman imparts service to every single member of her household, with the exclusion of herself.

***

At times, I felt as if I were peering up from the pitch-black bottom of a barrel and had all but vanished into thin air. *Emptiness permeated my soul. I lost my identity.* I had become so exhaustively engrossed in meeting the needs of others; I utterly neglected my own.

As strange as this may sound, many women have lost their identity in a similar fashion. I have found gratification in serving my family members, as well as others. But service should be provided in a healthy and well-balanced manner.

On numerous occasions, I allowed some of my children to manipulate me. At the time, it just seemed so much easier to give in to their selfish demands, rather than deal with the pain of their anger and rejection. Over time a couple of them actually became quite skillful at the game. For most children, it is merely human nature to insist on having their own way. *At whatever cost!* As parents, it is our responsibility to discourage their selfish and manipulative behaviors.

Dorothy Canfield Fisher wisely said, *"A mother is not a person to lean on but a person to make leaning unnecessary."*

***

Like cars driven for long distances without refueling, women who continually give of themselves without replenishing will soon be out of gas. Such behavior is predisposed to burnout; therefore, we should abstain from doing for others what they are capable of doing for themselves. Furthermore, God did not create a woman to exclusively and excessively serve others. While serving is a large part of a woman's life, it should not consume her.

I consider submission an admirable quality in a woman. Quite a few biblical women exemplified submission: Mary, Abigail, Esther, Ruth, and many others.

While Sarah is a close second, Hannah is the one who holds my greatest admiration. Both women pleased God. Sarah called her husband, Abraham, her lord and adorned herself with a meek and quiet spirit. Hannah was also submissive to her husband, Elkanah.

What impressed me most about Hannah? She was a woman of great faith. When Hannah was deeply troubled, she prayed and God answered.

As wives, many of us tend to lay our burdens on our husbands. But one of my greatest aspirations in life is to be more like Hannah.

In contrast, husbands demanding biblical submission club some wives over the head with scripture. But the Word of God admonishes us to submit to one another. And in the fifth chapter of Ephesians, husbands are told to love their wives as they love their own bodies.

God also commands the husband to love his wife in the same manner that Christ loves His Church. That's awesome love! And to the children, it states to, "Honor (esteem and value as precious) your father and your mother—this is the first commandment with a promise."

John Dryden said, *"God never made His work for man to mend."* Or women! Ladies, God did not put a boulder on your shoulder for you to single-handedly fix the world. We are God's workmanship and were created from love to be loved.

At times, some of us tend to feel taken for granted and unloved. Although such feelings may or may not be valid, nothing should prevent you from loving yourself. The first step in learning to implement self-love is to comprehend your self-worth.

Others (i.e., family members), who have become accustomed to your catering to their every demand, may not initially accept your spending more time on yourself. Therefore, arm yourself for an emotional power struggle and remain unswerving. Observers will only be convinced that you mean business after you have stayed consistent for a period of time.

When I put an end to excessively giving, I was accused (by a couple of my adolescents) of "jus' tripping". And asked, "What's up with you, lady?" or "Have you had your meds (prescription hormones) today?"

These were subtle disapprovals under the guise of jesting. The change will doubtless be dramatic for them as well, so expect some resistance.

Although some women want desperately to do all that is required of them, we cannot possibly be four to five different people simultaneously. What is more, when we fail to meet these unattainable expectations placed on us by others and ourselves, we often become self-condemning.

As a fanatical pleaser, I repeatedly ran myself into a state of physical and mental exhaustion. And then I gave myself a good old-fashion beating and retired into the evening wearing my dunce hat.

Some of my unattainable expectations were no doubt ingrained in me as a little girl. Among my favorite childhood television shows were "Leave it To Beaver" and "The Donna Reed Show". Those families ate dinner together, and the houses were immaculate. The kitchen floors were so shiny you could eat off them. And not only was June Cleaver the perfect mother and wife, she looked exceptional in her clean, crisp apron. But as I look back, I realize that even June Cleaver was a perfectionist.

I still struggle with perfectionism as it pertains to keeping my kitchen clean, but I am not nearly as driven. Those old programs were a wonderful source of entertainment, but they were also unrealistic. Perhaps back then, the wives were stay-at-home moms who cooked, cleaned, and baked cookies.

Women of the millennium are not likely to be June Cleaver. But on the other hand, June Cleaver would have also found it a great challenge to sport the hats of the millennium woman.

While enjoying some of my favorite television shows, I was actually setting myself up for perfectionism. Even though my mother had never pressured me to clean up, I would not go out to play without completing my household chores. One Saturday morning, I annoyingly stood at my mother's bed yelling at her as though the house was on fire. "Momma, Momma," I shouted, "Where's the broom, Momma?"

All I wanted to do was go out and play, and she wanted much-needed rest after a long workweek. But I refused to leave the house without sweeping our old wooden floors.

Needless to say (and understandably so), Momma was aggravated with my disruptive and persistent behavior. Sarcastically, she responded, "The broom is in my mouth."

With quick come back, I demanded that she spit it out so that I could sweep the floor.

The very next thing I remember was a sweep across my mouth with the back of her hand.

While a friend was visiting me one day, Momma gave her fair warning. She said, "Honey, you better move out of the way before Laurette sweeps you out of the door."

The cruel and inconsiderate way the kids ridiculed me about our old frame house augmented my obsession to keep it clean.

While cleanliness is a wonderful quality, all things should be done in moderation.

***

Rummaging through my wardrobe of hats, I found and dusted off my self-hat. And I wear it adoringly with pride. It looks fabulous on me, too, even if I must say so myself. Also, I am sporting my wife's hat, one I intend to wear for the rest of my life. The maid's hat will not be getting much wear; I will only be wearing it occasionally. And the dunce hat was burned at the stake.

While Wonder Woman's headpiece may be enviable, we must remember that she is only a myth. And there is no such thing as a super woman. As a matter of fact, Wonder Woman was not even a wonder woman.

Ladies, I suggest that we all run out and get ourselves a tiara, because no queen's attire is complete without one. Wear your crown in honor of all that you have been to so many people over the years. God knows it is time that we celebrate our successes, rather than continually brood over past failures.

***

While emerging from the bottom of my barrel, I realized that even at a mature age I was still not quite sure of what I wanted to be when I grew up (emotionally). Nearly half my life had been spent encouraging others to pursue their dreams and passions. But when I decided to pursue my own, I found them at the end of my long and drawn out "things to do," list.

As women, it is imperative to understand and appreciate that life is a personal gift from God. And we have been empowered with the potential to accomplish great things. Not just for others, but also for us.

In His Image

*A lump of clay,
a pile of colorless sand,
Lying formless
in a most magnificent hand.*

*One finger, two fingers,
three fingers, four,
Came down upon me
and pressed me sore.*

*Upwards I glanced,
how wondrous to see
My Potter's face
looking down at me.*

*How magnificent,
how gloriously divine,
Of His own image,
He did make me to shine.*

Take the Scenic Route

In today's world of "hurry up and get it done by yesterday", many of us rush through life without enjoying its scenic route. Like racecar drivers, some of us are speeding to complete one task so that we can take on the next. During these stressful times in which we are living, we must learn to enjoy life's scenic route.

While many of us are proficient multi-taskers, only a few women take the time to stop, look, and listen to the pleasantries of nature. Women have the uncanny ability to simultaneously apply make-up, drink coffee, and talk on the cellular phone while driving to work in the mornings. (I must confess I was guilty of all the above.)

In the evenings, I prepared wonderful dinners for my husband and myself. I took great pride in having a beautiful centerpiece arrangement, matching china, and cloth napkins. Willie, my husband, was generous with compliments and he would absolutely marvel over the delicious dinners that I had prepared ... as well as the beautiful table settings. We would have classy champagne glasses filled to the rim with chilled carrot juice, spiced with ginger.

After serving a delectable dinner, I sat down with my husband and said grace while chewing my first bite. Then I would immediately inhale the rest so that I could race over to the sink and clean the dishes. Meanwhile, Willie sat alone at the table, enjoying his evening meal. I, on the other hand, had no way of knowing how great it was; as I never took the time to actually taste the food I took great pleasure in preparing. They generally went past my taste buds and down into my stomach. I simply swallowed my food.

One particular evening, I remember actually standing over Willie as he ate his dinner and reaching for his plate to clear the table. To say that I was out of control is gravely understated. Annoyed with me - and understandably so, my darling beloved gaped at me as he unyieldingly protested, "Laurette I will not be in a hurry to finish my dinner."

Meaningful conversation was unattainable at the dinner table. Whenever we made an attempt to engage in a discussion, my husband rarely had my undivided attention. I was somewhat comparable to a VCR. My racing mind would either be rewinding to the past or fast-forwarding to the future. It was as though my play button was jammed, or I was always changing the channels. My instability had to have been extremely perplexing to my husband, since it was virtually impossible for him to talk with me.

Fast-forwarding through life appeared to be evident in everything that I did. For example, the decor in my bathroom offered serenity ... seemingly the ideal place to unwind after a stressful day. Aromatherapy oils, body splash, lotions, candles, and lots of other goodies decorated the counter in my bathroom. Mounted on the wall was an elegant green and white glass candleholder with lots of candles, a gift from my husband.

At dusk, I would make myself a nice cup of soothing herbal tea to sip slowly by candlelight. Then I would fill the bathtub with a generous amount of scented bubble bath and bath oil beads. After preparing a bath fit for a queen, I would jump in the tub, gulp down my tea and jump back out again. While I was still dripping wet, my husband often assisted me in drying my back, which I must confess was quite embarrassing. And to make matters worse, he would innocently ask, "Honey are you done with your bath already?"

I could not relax because I was always on a mission. And if I did not have a mission, it would become my mission to find one.

My constant failure to slow down and "take the scenic route" is what would cause me to consistently worry without merit.

One day a florist made a surprise delivery. My husband, being the love of my life, would always send me roses. However, this particular one was not only unique, but was also the most beautiful floral arrangement I had ever seen.

I almost ruined the moment by calling him and complaining, "Sweetheart why did you spend so much money, while we're on such a tight budget?"

The moment I heard myself speaking, I wished desperately that I could have caught the words and reeled them back into my mouth. But it was too late. The dam had broken and the water was falling.

The next morning after breakfast, Willie lit the fireplace, kissed me goodbye and was off to work. As I lay down to read near the blazing fire, I caught a whiff of the most wonderful fragrance from the exotic arrangement my husband had sent me the day before. In haste, I jumped up and called him to thank him for such a thoughtful gesture. Then I said to him, "Baby, I love and appreciate you so much".

We must never take life or our loved ones for granted, because no one knows what tomorrow holds. It's far better to give our loved ones too much than to give them too little.

At one point in my life, I received a life-threatening diagnosis from my doctor. This was a wake up call as well as an unfriendly reminder that our life does not always continue to a ripe, old age. Now, I am aware of not taking my loved one's for granted. And I am also learning to maximize each moment of my life, as well.

At the dawn of each day, I savor my herbal teas by sipping them slowly.

***

As I transitioned from merely existing to living high on life, my husband and I had relocated to Central Florida. We lived in an apartment home in the beautiful city of Orlando with a paradise of its own.

From the rear balcony, I often sat captivated by a symphony of ducks quacking, fish splashing and of birds chirping to the gentle background sounds of a waterfall. As the ducks swam in unison upon the pond, the birds fluttered carefree across the sky.

There was such harmony among the ducks; it was as though they were one big happy family. When one got out of the pond, the others followed. They swam, ate and slept together, and it was quite intriguing to see how peacefully they co-existed. From them I learned that we must embrace every opportunity we have to enjoy these pleasantries in life; otherwise they may be forever lost.

Being called a *birdbrain* carries a derogatory implication; nevertheless, I think there's a lot we can learn from birds. The Bible admonishes us to observe and consider the birds; in doing so, we may learn to live carefree lives. Luke 12:24, states "Observe and consider the ravens: for they neither sow nor reap, they have neither storehouse nor barn, and [yet] God feeds them. Of how much more worth are you than the birds! And which of you by being overly anxious and troubled with cares can add a cubit to his stature or a moment [unit] of time to his age [the length of his life]? If then you are not able to do such a little thing as that, why are you anxious and troubled with cares about the rest?"

***

We lived in Orlando three years, and then returned to the South Florida City of Greenacres in West Palm Beach. Living near the beach was a plus for us, since we both loved the ocean.

One Saturday morning (about 5:30 a.m.), my husband excitedly awakened me. I was sleepy but I obeyed, because his surprises are always worth losing a little sleep.

Wow! The surprise was breakfast at a restaurant over the ocean, where we ate while watching the sunrise. And I am sure words could describe how scrumptious the breakfast was, but I cannot think of any at the moment. The food was out of this world. My banana nut pancakes were topped with large walnuts and slices of bananas. Willie's blueberry pancakes were oozing with whole fresh blueberries. We also had scrambled eggs and bacon, sausage, and home fried potatoes.

Afterwards, we went off for a long stroll down the beach. It was great!

Enjoy your life; fill your heart with beauty so that when you are confronted with the potential stresses of life, they will not seem as weighty. God has given us the gift of life, and life's simple pleasures are the absolute best.

We live in a "microwave" society that screams out at us to trade in a quality life with our families for money. Too many women are working overtime on their jobs to accumulate more material possessions. While scores of children are eating fast foods and spending too much time at home alone.

Whenever possible, women should cut back on the pursuit of materialism and invest quality time with their children. Housewives should comprise a budget so that their husbands can spend more time at home as well.

Most people are in a hurry to make money, but are too exhausted to enjoy it. *A life of happiness is not determined by our many possessions, but rather by our quality of living.* Fancy restaurants are nice on special occasions, but I am delighted when my husband gets excited over the aroma that welcomes him to a delicious home-cooked meal. He often says, "Baby, when I smell that food, I say to myself 'Man, I hope that's coming from our kitchen'!"

Instant foods are both convenient and economical, but don't hang up your apron just yet and deny you or your family some old-fashioned home cooking. If you don't have a family, cook a meal for someone who's sick or shut in. Their appreciation will reward you in ways that would make it more than worth your while.

***

In times gone by, I was accustomed to reserving certain perfumes and outfits for special occasions. Every day that God blesses us with life is an occasion to be celebrated. All of our yesterdays are gone forever.

Enjoy a cup of herbal tea and take time to smell the roses. Put something (time, energy, love) into someone else's life; it can be both enriching and rewarding. Share a smile or a kind gesture.

Regardless of what it is, we all have something to give. Celebrate life as if it were your very own party, and treat others as your party guests.

Smell the Roses

Yesterday is gone forever;
tomorrow has not arrived.
Celebrate your life today;
thank God that you're alive.

Sip a cup of coffee slowly;
try a brand that's flavored
Take your time and taste it,
for coffee should be savored.

Enjoy the pleasantries of life;
don't be in such a hurry,
Tomorrow comes with it's own cares,
today we need not worry.

Body, Soul, & Spirit

Aerobics is a form of cardiovascular conditioning that works wonders for firming the hips, thighs, and stomach. While burning body fat is important to obtain optimal health, many women do it for appearances only.

Meanwhile, inside of a beautifully packaged body, the woman's soul may be filled with unresolved emotional issues. Although some women may have healthy bodies and souls, the spiritual part of their triune must also be considered. God made the body from the earth; it houses and transports the soul and the spirit. Therefore, it is of the utmost necessity that we maintain optimal physical health. As without the body to provide and accommodate them, the soul and the spirit cannot dwell in the earth.

Moreover, the soul animates (gives life to) the body and houses the mind, will, and emotions. The body has no life and is entirely unable to function without the soul. The spirit, which is the innermost part of our triune, is often referred to as the "inner man." The Holy Spirit dwells within our spirit (inner man) when we become born-again Christians. Without Him (the Holy Spirit), our bodies may be ambulatory, but we are spiritually dead and doomed to eternal destruction. To become healthy and fulfilled women, it is of the essence that we nurture our triune being in its entirety.

Since the body is the visible part of our trinity, it gets the majority of our attention. After splashing on costly perfumes, oils, and lotions, we adorn our bodies with designer apparel and elegant jewelry. Many of us have extensions (hair, nails, or breasts) protruding from diverse parts of our bodies. And piercing is no longer for the ears only; we now pierce our noses, belly buttons, tongues, and eye brows.

This may sound a bit redundant and perhaps humorous, but it's quite true that we go to great lengths to beautify ourselves. However, while the body is being superficially showcased, the soul and the spirit, which are the invisible parts of our triune, are generally the most neglected.

Genesis 1:26 states, "God said, Let Us [Father, Son, and Holy Spirit] make mankind in Our image, after Our likeness, and let them have complete authority over the fish of the sea, and the birds of the air, the [tame] beasts, and over all the earth, and over everything that creeps upon the earth." The scripture states that God is triune and we, as His creation, are also triune. We were made in the image of God. As the Father, Son, and Holy Spirit in unity created mankind to give us authority in the world, we must come together in unity — body, soul, and spirit — to exercise that authority given to us, over our lives.

To become completely fulfilled women; we must first seek God, who offers us the gift of eternal life through salvation. It is the single, most important gift that we will ever be given in life. When we accept God's gift of salvation, we then become spiritually healthy. Romans 10:10 states, "For with the heart a person believes (adheres to, trusts in, and relies on Christ) and so is justified (declared righteous, acceptable to God), and with the mouth he confesses (declares openly and speaks out freely his faith) and confirms [his] salvation."

Simply confess that Jesus is the Son of God, invite Him into your heart, and you will experience a peace that exceeds human comprehension. Salvation (spiritual rebirth), is the most important because the soul and spirit will live on, while the body will eventually return to the earth. Again, salvation or the lack thereof, will determine where we will spend our eternity.

Women, get to work on the soul of your triune, which is the healing of the emotions. Having been subjected to abuse, the mind must be renewed (changed) with the word of God, which is practical and timeless. Read God's word and apply it, with the full assurance that the Holy Spirit will help you to be restored. Depending upon the severity of your emotional injury, you may need Christian counseling, which is offered by most churches free of charge.

Dealing with the soul (emotions) of your triune may also require you to re-visit the gravesites of some hurtful experiences that were buried prematurely. So, get busy brushing away the dust and the cobwebs of tombstones, which may possibly expose the names of sexual, verbal, physical, or emotional abuse.

In one of the tombs may lie sexual abuse; here you may find buried memories of sexual violations. Family members, (brothers, uncles, and fathers) may have sexually assaulted their sisters, nieces, and daughters. Trusted friends of the family have sexually violated many young girls. Regardless of who the offender may have been, the victim commonly feels guilty and buries the painful memories.

Engraved on the next tombstone may be physical abuse, which is often used, as a form of discipline, but it is distinctively different. Discipline should be applied with love to correct the child's actions ... solely for the good of the child. Physical abuse, on the other hand, is administered out of anger and frustration, with a willful and deliberate intent to inflict pain. The various instruments (sticks, electrical cords, wire hangers, or other objects) that may have been used for disciplinarian purposes were unquestionably abusive. More often than not, parents who were abused during their childhood years abuse their children.

Leaves and debris blown away from the slab at yet another gravesite may disclose the engravings, "Here laid to restlessness is Verbal Abuse." In this particular grave you may have buried harsh and demeaning words that stripped you of your self-worth. As inhumane as physical abuse may be, verbal abuse in most cases is just as debilitating. Although the majority of physical scars heal, most of the verbal abuse scars are emotionally and mentally crippling and may remain with you throughout your life.

Grab a shovel from the tool shed and dig up those dilapidated gravesites. It's time to quiet the echoes of the longtime haunting voices that have plagued your soul. Only then will you be freed from grief, anger, and misplaced guilt.

It may help to confront the person who has caused you such deep pain, if this poses no threat to you.

Forgiveness is imperative for emotional freedom and peace of mind. Ask God to help you to forgive. He understands your pain and His love for you is immeasurable. Hebrews 4:15 states, "For we do not have a High Priest Who is unable to understand and sympathize and have a shared feeling with our weakness and infirmities and liability to the assaults of temptation, but One Who has been tempted in every respect as we are, yet without sinning."

Never once did Jesus yield to the temptation of unforgiveness, even against those who brutally abused Him. Embodied in human flesh, Jesus suffered excruciating pain at the hands of His abusers. But had God not given His Son to forgive the sins of the world, we all would be hopelessly lost forever. He is a present help for us, even during those times we find it difficult to forgive. We must allow Jesus to be our example. As He has forgiven us, we must also forgive others.

Although forgiveness is a key factor to your healing, making your abuser accountable is also important. Notifying the proper authorities does not demonstrate unforgiveness, but this act does exemplify taking responsible actions.

After you have made peace with your past, give your experiences their proper burial. As whole individuals, we can better love ourselves and make sound decisions.

When our emotionally damaged soul undergoes restoration, we then become like the woman in Proverbs

31, whose worth is *far above jewels*.

Then, put on some track shoes and go running. Physical fitness will take on a new meaning now that you have become spiritually and emotionally healthy. Eat nutritious foods and drink plenty of water. For a real nutritional boost, juice and drink fruits and vegetables, 2 to 3 times a week. Get the proper amount of rest and exercise, along with regular checkups, and your body will reward you for all your efforts.

If you are experiencing a lack of peace, a feeling of emptiness, or constant fatigue, you may be neglecting an essential part of yourself. In my process of connecting and nurturing my body, soul, and spirit, I feel significantly better than I have ever felt in my entire life. It is exciting and adventurous, and I am enjoying every anticipated moment of my journey.

God made us triune, and every part of us is designed with a unique purpose. When we are good stewards over what God has given us, it pleases Him. And He rewards us with peace, prosperity, and long life in accordance with His purpose.

Body, Soul, Spirit

When I connect with myself,
it's then that I'm whole,
In harmony I must agree
in spirit, body, and soul.

More than meets the naked eye,
so much more to me,
Body, Soul, and Spirit,
not one of me, but three.

My soul will live forever,
My body's passing through,
My spirit is eternal,
just two of me won't do.

God first formed my body,
then to make me whole
He breathed in me a spirit,
and added to me a soul.

Happy on Purpose

A woman is the spiritual aspiration of her home; when she's unhappy, so are the other family members. Although emotional pain can be excruciating, we can respond with bitterness or *betterness*. After we have endured the insufferable pain of abuse, we can travel one of two roads: the road of forgiveness (where there is healing and peace) or the road of prolonged anger and unforgiveness (where there is torment and unrest).

Horace wrote, *"Anger is a momentary madness, so control your passion or it will control you"*.

An angry, unforgiving woman often spends her entire life inflicting pain on her husband, children, and all others she meets. Her bite can be venomous, and she has an insatiable appetite to destroy. Proverbs 12:4 states that a virtuous and worthy wife [earnest and strong in character] is a crowning joy to her husband, but she who makes him ashamed is as rottenness in his bones."

Raging anger boils over out of the soul like lava from the peak of a volcano. Both are dangerous and may even prove to be deadly. The vilest crimes have been committed by people who later declared momentary insanity. It seems that such volatile anger is often the infusion of unrelented bitterness, unforgiveness, and resentment. All are dormant emotions that may explode at any time quite unexpectedly.

When a woman's heart is consumed by rage, love is often an unwelcome entity. Rest flees from her presence and restlessness becomes her constant companion. Overshadowed by oppression and darkness, she allows sorrow to consume her unhappy home like a tornado would a city. Her misery is immeasurable.

Joseph Addison said, *"A misery is not to be measured from the nature of the evil, but from the temper of the sufferer."*

What has long been stated in the Bible is now being scientifically proven. Stress is one of the major causes of cancer and other health-related issues. Proverbs 15:13 proclaims, "A glad heart makes a cheerful countenance, but by sorrow of the heart the spirit is broken".

Embitterment is a waste of precious time, health and — in some instances — its victim's life. For a woman to infuriate herself in a vengeful attempt to destroy others is unhealthy and unproductive. Metaphorically speaking, some enraged women walk around with boulders on their shoulders. Many of them actually feel justified wallowing in their own agony and misery. Most women have dealt with pain, grief, and maltreatment in life; however, to become self-satisfied with victimization is self-defeating. Often women who have been emotionally wounded forbid their hearts to heal.

Scourging was a method of punishment that generally preceded the crucifixion of an alleged criminal in the days of the Roman Empire. The leather whip that was used for scourging had several thongs, each weighed with sharp pieces of metal to tear into the victim's flesh. Due to the severity of such punishment, some people actually died before they were crucified. But when faced with scourging and crucifixion, Jesus (who was innocent), knowing the unjustifiable humiliation and indescribable pain that He was about to endure for us (who were guilty), still found it in His heart to pray, "Father, forgive them, for they know not what they do."(Luke 23:34).

Have you ever been scourged or faced crucifixion? What excuse do you have to hold onto unforgiveness? We are entirely without excuse, since our excuses were nailed to the cross with Jesus, our Supreme example of forgiveness.

***

Despite their life's hardships, Abigail, Esther, and Ruth made quality decisions to journey down the road of forgiveness and peace. Each of their lives had the essence of a fairytale ending. They all had the right attitude about life and refused to wallow in pools of bitterness. As a result, their endings were better than their beginnings.

Abigail was, no doubt, unhappily married to Nabal, whom the Bible records as crude and boring. Some of us know firsthand (others as spectators) that whether it is the husband or the wife, marriage to a miserable, self-loathing individual is no picnic. Abigail was gracious, beautiful, and kindhearted. She was the bomb! (The story of this magnificent creature is beautifully portrayed in I Samuel 25, and I have yet to read it with dry eyes). In due course, the wise Abigail did get her knight in shining armor.

It all started when the gallant David (who was to become King of Israel) journeyed to the wilderness of Maon, the home of the wealthy, but wickedly dishonest Nabal. David and his men had been unselfishly accommodating to Nabal's men during their travels. And now that the shoe was on the other foot, David had hoped that while he and his men were in Nabal's neck of the woods, Nabal might extend the same courtesy.

David sent some of his men to kindly request provision from Nabal, who predictably and harshly refused. When word got back to David, he was angered to the point of killing him and his entire family. David had no tolerance for an egocentric man like Nabal.

Apparently, neither man knew the other very well. Perhaps the upcoming king who had shown kindness did not expect the rich man to *figuratively* look down his nose at him. And perhaps the rich Nabal had no idea that the combatant David would unsheathe his sword and desire to remove his nose from his face!

Abigail truly exemplified the woman in Proverbs 14: "Every wise woman builds her house, but the foolish one tears it down with her own hands." Had she not exercised her God-given wisdom, she and the others would have suffered a mass execution.

After hearing how her husband had endangered his family

by his foolhardy refusal of David, Abigail acted swiftly. She gathered up some servants and took two hundred loaves of bread, wine, raisin cakes, sheep, and corn to David in an attempt to appease his anger.

Throughout history, women in an attempt to be equal to men, have lost touch with their femininity. Women are not supposed to be equal to men, nor can we match their physical strength. We are not above or beneath them—just plain and simply by God's design *different.*

The feminine attributes that women have were not dishonorably given to us. And yet the enemy who has set out to destroy the family structure has deceived many into believing such a lie. As a result, some women have become hardened, bitter, and controlling.

But Abigail's femininity extinguished David's fiery temper. She approached David and lay prostrate before him. She then apologized for her husband's ill-mannered behavior and pleaded for David's forgiveness. If she had gone out to have a verbal (rubber necking) altercation with him, my guess is she would not have gotten very far.

Furthermore, had Abigail been an embittered wife because of Nabal, she would have missed the opportunity to save her life and many others. But because she was full of light and not darkness, the Lord ordered her footsteps. (I Samuel 35) "So David accepted what she had brought him and said to her, go up in peace to your house. See I have hearkened to your voice and have granted your petition."

The Bible says that a soft answer turns away anger. Ten days after this encounter, Nabal died and David became Abigail's knight in shining armor. He married her because she found favor with him.

***

In the book of Esther, King Ahasuerus divorced Queen Vasti, who was beautiful but needed an attitude adjustment. The king later married Esther, who was submissive.

After the deaths of both her parents, her father's nephew Mordecai reared Hadassah (better known as Esther). She wasn't bitter over the deaths of her parents but was a beautiful woman inside and out.

Mordecai was influential in getting Esther into the king's court, where she later became Queen Esther. Anyone entering the king's court without being summoned was put to death. When Queen Esther desired to enter, although she had not been invited, King Ahasuerus extended his golden scepter, bidding her entrance. And, get this: he also offered her anything she wanted ... even half of his kingdom!

Queen Esther had the right attitude; she handled her business and found favor with the king.

***

The Book of Ruth was also inspired by the life of a woman who had the opportunity to be bitter. Ruth, a Moabite, was married to Mahlon, the son of Elimelech and Naomi. Ruth's husband, her brother-in-law, and her father-in-law all died within a short time span. But even in the sorrow of widowhood, Ruth made the quality decision to reject bitterness. Instead, she seized upon the opportunity to give her devotion and allegiance to her mother-in-law, Naomi. Her love and obedience to Naomi eventually led to her marriage to Boaz. And Ruth later gave Naomi a grandson, who became the grandfather of David and was in the lineage of Jesus Christ.

Had these women chosen to be victimized by their sorrow, their lives would have taken different courses.

***

Diamond in the Rough is my memoir; it surpasses my life's story and enters the realm of mentorship. Each chapter denotes pain and suffering. My father abandoned me, and I grew up without the emotional support of my mother.

At sixteen, I was pregnant and married to a man who physically abused me throughout our marriage. When I was seventeen, my mother was brutally killed; a year later, my first-born son died. Later on, I was divorced and remarried three times to men who were abusive, unfaithful, and eventually walked out of my life. I was brutally beaten at knifepoint by an attempted rapist, who left me bruised and bloody. I have been homeless, rejected, abused and neglected.

Additionally, I was diagnosed with an Acoustic Neuroma lodged at the base of my brain and told that it may possibly be fatal.

I think you probably get my point by now. When I instruct you to deal with pain and anger and move onto happiness and peace, I believe that I am qualified to make such a statement.

Life is too short to spend it any other way than in the pursuit of true happiness. What will you take to your grave? An angry, bitter, unforgiving heart or a life illuminated with love, happiness, and forgiveness?

Happiness is a choice. It's highly contagious and people are often enthusiastically infected by it. Beware of the side effects, which is the feeling of walking high spirited on cloud nine. James Oppenhelm said, *"The foolish man seeks happiness in the distance, the wise grows it under his feet."*

A seed of happiness that's planted and cultivated in the mind eventually spreads like a wildflower throughout the entire realm of the emotions.

Unforgiveness is toxic to the soul. If you have been clinging to unforgiveness it is time for a change. Seek God's forgiveness about your unforgiveness. (To feel justified with your unforgiveness means to be self-assured that you have never needed to be forgiven.)

Be happy on purpose. Anything short of happiness is a waste of time, and who has time to waste? Proverbs 31 asks, "A capable, intelligent, and virtuous woman, who is he who can find her?"

Happy

H is for happiness, a choice of the will
A is for anger, a disease that can kill
P is for purpose; Christ died on the cross
P is for priceless, His life for the lost
Y is for yield your unforgiveness to Him;
as He died for you, He died for them.

Fair Maiden and her Prince

(a different Cinderella story)

Once upon a time, there was a delightful fair maiden who was beautiful but dirt poor. The maiden had spent most of her life dreaming of one day beholding a dark, delicious, and debonair prince.

But the poor maiden had had a streak of bad luck while in pursuit of her dream lover. Just as she was on the verge of giving up, WOW! There he was, with snow-white teeth that sparkled like diamonds against his black satiny completion. Even the maiden's dreams did not do her prince justice. Her eyes danced and glistened with sheer delight as they welcomed the wonderful sight of him.

* * *

In my favorite fairytale, one that almost everyone knows, Cinderella's Prince Charming rescued her from a repulsive step-mom and two jealous stepsisters. After the sudden death of her father, who was a widower, she was made a servant in her own home, and waited on her obnoxious extended family hand and foot. The story ends with Cinderella eventually marrying Prince Charming, and they moved into his palace where they happily spend the rest of their lives together.

However, in this particular story, the fair maiden's prince rescued her from the hood and a string of abusive relationships. But the poor maiden had no way of knowing the hardships and the disappointments she and her prince would encounter in their life together. And, while, happily ever after should be reserved strictly for fairy tales, this prince was indeed the love of her life.

Unlike any other fairytale that has ever been written, the fair maiden's story is for real. After the death of her mother, the young maiden was hurled out onto the stormy seas of life to either sink or swim. She was indeed fair to look upon, but she had had no prior life experiences to help her stay afloat. So before very long, the maiden plummeted to the ocean's floor and fell prey to sea scavengers. She embarked on a string of broken relationships with them.

All the while, the dispirited maiden was being continually stripped of her self-worth, and she seemed to have been meandering without purpose through life. While in pursuit of love, she woefully conceived and brought five children into her insufferable world.

Each relationship left her feeling a little more tainted and impure than the previous one. Her heart was filled with pain, anguish, and rejection. Be that as it may, instead of relenting, with fervor she sought even more for the prince who would rescue her from an unpleasant roller coaster ride.

One dismal day, the disgruntled maiden plopped down on her living room recliner. Swept away with emotional pain, she had become quite disenchanted with her life. When all at once she burst into tears.

"Oh God," she cried, "I feel so alone and unloved. Sometimes I don't think it possible for anyone to love someone like me."

Suddenly her piercing pain was gently replaced with serenity and calm. As God's small still voice spoke to her heart saying, "My daughter I love you."

Stinging, salty tears rushed down her face locking beneath her chin. At last! Her longtime pursuit of a prince actually led her to the Prince of Peace (Jesus).

God's infinite love permeated her heart and was incredibly gratifying ... but totally unfamiliar. Unlike Cinderella whose father loved her immeasurably, the maiden had only known a father who left her with a string of broken promises. But her heavenly Father was dependable, and His affirming presence was always with her. Unbeknownst to her, God's nurturing love was what she had pursued all along. It took immortal God, not mortal man to fill her void. And yet receiving the gift of salvation did not seem to immediately change her lifestyle, or so she thought.

The maiden's misguided perception of salvation lead her to believe that the moment she received it, all her problems would vanish at once. But little did she know while salvation is instantaneous, breaking her preexisting behavioral patterns would happen over a period of time. Unlike Cinderella's fairy godmother, God is not (always) in the zapping business. However, He would empower her with all that she needed on her journey to recovery.

Meanwhile, in her beautiful thrift store dresses, the maiden and her children were off to church every Sunday morning. She worked overtime to live up to her newfound faith. Despite her *religious* efforts, she continued to live the lifestyle that was familiar. Like water seeping through cracks of a broken cistern, God's love slowly trickled out of her broken soul. She was a real work in progress, and had not yet learned to transfer her dependency from man to God.

Before very long, God would teach the maiden to depend solely upon Him, and send her a prince of His own making. And the two of them would share a lifelong healthy relationship together.

The infamous Humpty Dumpty had fallen from a wall and was visibly shattered. Likewise, the maiden was broken and although not visibly, her lifestyle was evidence of her shattered emotions. All the king's horses and all the king's men could not put Humpty Dumpty together again. Fortunately for the maiden, she was now in God's hands, and putting people back together is His specialty.

The fair maiden married a second time and third time to men who were not only abusive, but also walked out of her life. In retrospect, she learned their leaving was a blessing in disguise, because she lacked the emotional health to leave them. But even if she had sent them away, *God would not have been pleased with me,* she honestly thought. And regardless to how abusive the relationships were, it was her bed of nails to sleep upon. After all, she had often heard divorce taught as though it were the unpardonable sin. *How dare they judge me?* Were the thoughts racing through her mind as she sat uncomfortably on the church's pew. *They're people of God. Can't they see that I need help?*

Then reality struck like a bolt of lightening with the fourth marriage, and the maiden knew she was in desperate need of help. That was it. She had bottomed out. The co-dependency addiction had taken its final toll.

Her fourth husband was not only unfaithful, but had struggled with a drug addiction for the entire four years of their marriage. The gripping fear for her health and the well being of her children continually plagued her. Nevertheless, she continued to work relentlessly on her marriage, because she thought it would *please* God.

***

Co-dependent addicts (co-ads) are individuals with diminished self-worth; they strive for the affirmation and approval of others. They have a diminutive opinion of themselves, and some seek their identity from their accomplishments and accolades.

Moreover, society at large labels a woman who is a codependent addict as promiscuous. But while the effect of her lifestyle may have the appearance of promiscuity, the cause is codependency.

The Bible gives a picturesque scene of a woman who is a (co-ad) in John, chapter 4. When Jesus met the Samaritan woman at the well, He said to her, "Everyone who drinks of this water shall thirst again; but whoever drinks of the water that I shall give him shall never thirst; but the water that I shall give him shall become in him a well of water springing up to eternal life."

The Samaritan woman, thirsty for love, had married five times to quench her thirst and was living with the sixth man. But her longing was insatiable.

***

There was similarity in the lifestyles of the fair maiden and the Samaritan woman, but both their lives were changed after meeting the Messiah. He gave them living water (salvation) so that they would never thirst again.

***

As the story goes on, the distraught maiden rode down the street one day crying and gasping for her breath. "Dear God, I don't want to cause shame to your name with these broken relationships and marriages."

Again her tears where quieted by His still small voice. "When you are emotionally crippled, you can not make a sound judgment. But when you are emotionally sound, a sound judgment will be required of you. My desire for you is our fellowship and your restoration."

Another weekend had approached and the maiden visited a church in her neighborhood. Routinely, she rushed home after service, in hopes of getting her house in order. However, on this particular day she felt strongly compelled to visit her former place of worship. Since her house was already in shambles, she decided (at least for that moment) it was time to pull herself together and get on with her life.

Service was already in session when she arrived. The maiden was a sight to behold in her beige dress covered with multi-shades of green leaves, and matching beige pumps. Her makeup was flawless; the natural sun streaks blended well with her sandy brown hair. Not to disturb anyone, she made her way quickly and quietly to one of the only two seats available in the front of the church.

Once the maiden had settled in, she was astonished by the profound sermon that the minister was teaching. Never before had she heard the word taught with such clarity and articulation. The minister's sermon was both informative and encouraging. Like a soothing ointment, it comforted her aching heart.

Who is he? She pondered with elation, and after the religious fog dissipated from her eyes, she noticed that he was as handsome as he was gifted.

After delivering the sermon, the minister came and sat in the empty seat next to hers. *Why did she feel paralyzed?* This mystified her, since she had no idea who he was, or why he had had such an impact on her.

During the pastor's closing remarks and acknowledgments, she learned the minister's name was Willie. After service she nervously shook his hand, thanked him for a wonderful message, and hurried home to the chaos that she knew awaited her.

Two Sundays later, the bemused maiden stood at the screen door watching as the church van dropped off her teenage daughter. To her amazement, there was the minister, once again driving the church van. He had joined and become an active member of the small outreach ministry. He caught a glimpse of her standing in the doorway, and saw the same illuminating beauty that he had seen previously in church. Breathing heavily and perspiring profusely, he attempted to wave calmly. She waved back, inconspicuously watching as the church van drove away.

***

Okay, by now I am sure you have figured out that I am the fair maiden, so I will continue telling my (real life) fairy tale. During the course of my recovery, I learned the hard way that it was not pleasing at all to God that I remain in an abusive relationship. Actually, it was an emotional deficiency that had me both driven and bound. I had never witnessed first hand a healthy marital relationship. All the married people I knew personally were at each other's throat most of the time. The only couples that were not fighting were the ones I saw on television.

There are couples who have been blessed with the experience of a traditional, one-time marriage. Unfortunately, such marriages seem to be vastly decreasing to a smaller percentage. Personally, couples who have been privileged with such marriages should be less judgmental of others who have not. Honestly, some of the messages that I heard made me feel hopeless, isolated, and alone.

***

Later, I rejoined my former place of worship and overtime became overwhelmingly attracted to Willie. Like a breath of fresh air, it was *Different! Innovative! Refreshing!* This was unlike any of the co-dependent feelings I had experienced in the past.

After having pondered these feelings for several months, I decided to call and ask Willie to meet me, so that I could express my feelings. We met at a Denny's restaurant in Hallandale, Florida. Nervously and clumsily, I blurted out what I felt and not so surprisingly he felt the same way about me.

We visited the most exquisite nature park one still, humid day. Standing under a tree limb, we looked into each other's eyes and vowed to forever share our love. Suddenly, the limb above us began to shake vigorously ... *but there was no wind blowing.*

We sat cuddled on a wooden park bench and discussed future plans.

One day while at work, Willie called and asked me to meet him at Denny's. It was the same restaurant in

Hallandale, where we had our first cup of coffee, and confessed our love almost one year prior. This seemed an odd request, seeing as there were many Denny's locally, in Fort Lauderdale.

Immediately after work, I retouched my makeup and hastened to meet him.

When I arrived, I found him seated and looking as handsome as ever with a huge smile on his face. Curiously, I sat across from him and gazed into his eyes as we shared pleasantries.

Before long, the waiter rushed over to take our order.

"What will you be having today?" He jovially asked.

Willie responded, "Bring me something special."

Mulling over his order I thought to myself, *what an odd request*. But Willie had prearranged with the staff at Denny's for my back to be turned away from the waiter so that I would not see him as he approached.

Walking up from behind, the waiter was carrying a tray with a beautiful bronze sculpture of two arms. The man's arm was attired in a tuxedo sleeve, while the woman's was graced with lace. And two of his fingers were placing a ring on hers. Hanging from one of his other fingers was a black velvet bag containing a dazzling diamond engagement ring.

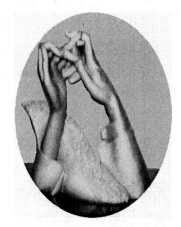

After the waiter placed the breathtakingly gorgeous statuette in front of me, Willie took my hand into his and asked "Darling, will you marry me?"

Through teary eyes I glanced up to find the entire restaurant, along with Willie awaiting my response. We had spoken at length about getting married, but in my wildest imagination I never dreamed of such a unique and romantic proposal.

And being that my momma didn't raise no fool, with much enthusiasm I shouted out an emphatic "Yes"!

There was an outburst of applause, and an elderly couple hastily made their way over to our table. The lady said with glee, "I hope your marriage will be as long and happy as ours has been."

Her husband who was smiling from ear to ear cheerfully added, "We have been married for over thirty years."

There was such romance in the air. The spectators were almost as excited as we were. They seemed to genuinely appreciate sharing our historical moment of our commitment to consummate our union.

In honor of our upcoming wedding, the manager sent over two complimentary glasses of wine.

***

Our festive wedding celebration was held on February 17, 1996, aboard a dinner cruise line. There had been some exceptionally cold weather in Florida. Willie and I prayed for suitable weather, so that I could wear my stunning wedding dress without an overcoat. As well, we wanted a perfect climate for the wedding cruise.

Behold! On the day of our wedding, God honored our request and miraculously changed the weather to a perfect climate. Special friends and family joined us. In fact, most of the people on board joined in our merriment.

Prince Willie and I were attractively attired in perfectly matching cream colored outfits. Scott McClintock designed my wedding dress, which would not have been more beautiful had Cinderella's fairy godmother zapped it herself. It was a chic, backless halter style dress, with floral embroidery and a mandarin-like collar that fastened around the neck with two pearl buttons. It looked much like a Chinese Cheongsam, and had an above the waist jacket. To compliment the dress, my hair was pulled back in a chignon, with a specially designed hairpiece made with tiny gold balls, baby's breath and fern. (Initially the hairpiece seemed a perplexing request, but the florist designed it exactly as I had envisioned. And the gold balls matched my purse and gold heels [i.e. glass slippers].)

Prince Willie was most charming. In real life or fairy tales, he was the grandest prince of all. His suit hung handsomely on his precise physique and was incredibly eye-catching. The barber's clippers had no doubt been sprinkled with angel's dust, because his haircut was heavenly.

Strolling hand in hand through the port as we approached the cruise ship, a banner waved overhead to the on boarding passengers, "Welcome to the Johnson's wedding."

One lady passenger said to me, "I hope you don't mind me saying, but your husband looks gorgeous."

I simply nodded my head in agreement, because what she saw, I had already seen in him.

My darling beloved made all the arrangements with the travel agent and it was truly a night of bliss and romance. Although our wedding was not terribly expensive, it was both memorable and priceless. We had a fabulous time with our friends and enjoyed a most flavorsome dinner.

The effigy of a black bride and groom stood stately on top of the multitiered cake. Soon after cutting the cake, we entered the dance floor and cut the rug. Then off to our cabin we went to toast champagne as we sat gazing out the window.

Willie rented an ocean's view cabin; had it not been for the window, we could have reached out and touched the water. (I blush as I confess we got more than our money's worth.)

As we celebrated our wedding night, I fell asleep in the arms of my Prince Charming.

At midnight, the clock chimed. It was time for Cinderella to leave the ball. But the loud sound of vacuum cleaners signaled to the fair maiden and her prince that it was time to disembark the ship. Other than the cleaning crew, we were the only passengers on board.

We jumped up and quickly got dressed. Just as Cinderella's coach turned back into a pumpkin, the weather had once again turned bitingly cold. When we found our best man, he was shivering with folded arms. Soon after, we met up with our other guest who wanted to know where had we been. Everyone else had gotten off the ship!

* * *

In addition to our fairy tale wedding, we shared other pleasurable times enjoying the ocean and its beauty. We often ate seafood while lying near the water, strolled the boardwalk or danced in the street to the music of live bands. Other times we climbed up in the lifeguard's booth—casting our cares upon the waters (relinquishing our burdens to God).

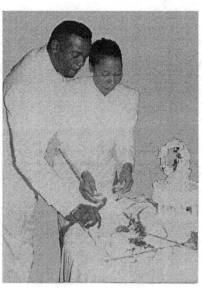

Later we shared a grand honeymoon on a cruise to Freeport, Bahamas, aboard a wonderful cruise line. *That's another story!*

Our fairy tale life together has included a wonderful nine years of marital bliss. And although this is a different kind of Cinderella story, it is mine and I am sharing it with my prince, who is indeed the love of my life.

My Prince

*My Prince, indeed,
is the love of my life,
I am blessed and
 honored
to be his wife.*

*He holds me close
under moonlit skies,
I only see romance
when I look in his eyes.*

*He's strong and yet gentle,
 he's loving and kind
Charming and handsome,
he stays on my mind*

*Euphoric with his kiss,
 hypnotized by his charm
Utopia is mine,
when he holds me in his arms*

*My Prince on earth,
truly my greatest love
Comes second to none
but my Prince up above.*

Diamond in the Rough

Laurette Taylor Johnson